To AIR is Human

AVIATION ADVENTURES & ANECDOTES

Ray Thiele

OLOMANA PUBLISHERS

TO **AIR** IS HUMAN

AVIATION ADVENTURES & ANECDOTES
COMPILED BY RAY THIELE

Produced by Olomana Publishers
SAN: 298-4016
1605 Uluamahi Place
Kailua, Hawaii 96734

ISBN: O-9643365-1-0

Cover Design and Illustrations by the
author
Typesetting & Layout by P. C. Russell

Library of Congress Catalogue Card
Number:
96-69166

First edition

This book dedicated
to the indomitable
personnel of the
U. S. Navy's
PATROL BOMBING SQUADRON 128
who served with distinction
over the Atlantic & Pacific Oceans
during World War II

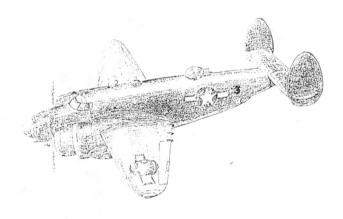

TABLE OF CONTENTS

Chapter 1   **In the Beginning**   **Page 11**
The Wright brothers; France's Louis Blériot...

Chapter 2   **Learning While Yearning**   **Page 17**
Looking at aviation from a beginner's viewpoint

Chapter 3   **In the Days of Yore... The DC-3**   **Page 31**
The fabulous Douglas DC-3 airliner & stories..

Chapter 4   **To Really Get There..**   **Page 43**
The history of air navigation & assorted tales
of those who did and didn't get there

Chapter 5   **The Military: *Not* a Piece of Cake**   **Page 57**
But the best of them survive

Chapter 6   **Some People Get the Word..**   **Page 85**
The hard way.. or with cigars.. or orchids..

Chapter 7   **Sexual Harassment?.. *Naaah***   **Page 99**
The games pilots played. Innocent bedevilment?

Chapter 8   **To Each His Own**   **Page 111**
The spice of life with alert people

Chapter 9   **To Ghana With Love**   **Page 125**
"What?..No bottles?.. no beer"

Chapter 10 **The Airline's Talent**   **Page 133**
Flight/attendants—the paradox of PR & safety

Chapter 11 **Skill Will Out**   **Page 143**
But luck—good or bad—plays a part

Chapter 12 **Ground to Air and Back Again**   **Page 157**
A strange mix of experiences

Chapter 13 **Forgive Us Our Trespasses**   **Page 169**
Pressures, problems and pranks

FOREWORD

While the Wright brothers flew the first successful powered aircraft in 1903, in earlier years there were men having visions of rising birdlike; of soaring to the clouds; looking down upon earthbound humans. But since those first pioneer flights, it has become obvious thousands of mortals have eagerly sought opportunities through aviation.

To be airborne has become a very people-type event.

In short: to air is human.

The author was an aviator for 42 years, twenty-five of which were spent in Hawaii. As if the first part of that statement wasn't sufficiently joyful, the last part proved meaningful in itself, for Hawaiians try to keep humor in most of what they do.

That attitude prompted the writer to seek stories about events that could help engender happiness. In general, you will find the author's intentions were reasonably successful, but some inject a note of sadness or point up the hazards of flight, others try to broaden non-fliers' knowledge of what the aviation world has been all about.

For the truly uninitiated, aeronauts—as professional as most have been—wound up carrying every earthly trait to unbounded heights; humor and practical jokes included. Even during the occasional tragedy and the seriousness of the operational process, a strange or odd sense of humor invariably developed after the fact.

Perhaps in the early days, aviation's potential for catastrophic dangers taught aviators that smiles and laughter kept "ol' debbil fear" from creeping in.. much like the rider having been bucked off a horse now has to overcome future anxiety by climbing right back in the saddle.

So the author intended to reflect the humor all of us experienced during our individual ventures in the flying game. A few more serious items were added to give the non-aviation oriented readers an insight into the lives of people who are, or were, a part of the world of flight.

But often in this competitive, pressure-packed world, the fun times found in yesterday's aerial industry have also gradually been diminishing. There is little place for the gags and games of years gone by. Certainly within the aerial machine, because the need for maximum safety in the precision-based skies of today is paramount.

And there is little evidence pranks in the airplane or spacecraft still exist, but looking back at one that occurred fifty years ago must have scared even the most "cool cat" aboard.

This happened in a Douglas DC-4 airliner flying passengers across the southwestern United States. Flight conditions were good and the air was smooth, leaving the passengers free of seat-belt restraint. In addition to the normal crew, one of the airline's flight inspectors ("check pilot") was sitting in the cockpit slightly aft but between the two pilots.

To the cockpit crew, the long flight had apparently gotten boring. The pilots had placed the flight controls on automatic pilot. But within the previous fifteen minutes, the captain had observed the automatic pilot wasn't doing its normal job. Despite the captain's repeated usage of corrective action that should have brought the aircraft nose down, the plane's altitude slowly crept higher and higher. Finally the continued use of the "nose down" trim tab reached the end of its range. It was full down, yet there was no change in the aircraft's tendency to continue creeping higher.

Initially puzzled, the captain ultimately discovered the reason. The plane's gust lock was on, done so as a gag by the check pilot. With the gust lock on, all of the aircraft's flight control surfaces were immovable, denying any of the pilots, automatic or otherwise, the option of maneuvering the airplane!

When the captain instinctively reached over and removed the gust lock control, the aircraft just previously "trimmed" to a full nose down position, was now free to react, and did so with a vengeance! With release of the gust lock, the nose suddenly pitched sharply forward and into what fliers call an outside loop!

Some gag!!

Fortunately, the copilot was still strapped to his seat and wasn't up against the ceiling with everybody else. He saved the day at the bottom of that loop by rolling the aircraft to an attitude of being 'right side up.' Fortunately, too, the Douglas airliner survived the violence of a fierce acrobatic maneuver it was never designed to perform.

And the check pilot who played the trick was fired faster than greased lightning goes through cardboard.

Save us from an experience like that! Totally foreign to the attitudes and actions of any check pilots in today's world.

For years the excitement and enthusiasm of being a part of aviation have kept the writer intrigued with the many stories that will result from any long career. Collecting them has become a habit, but having missed or forgotten so many, it was necessary to scout through the memories of a large number of friends and associates.

Obviously all of the tales you find here didn't happen to the author alone. Some are even before his time in this world—almost ancient history itself. Some are from experiences in a civilian flight school more than 55 years ago; others from the Navy's flight program; one or two from corporate pilots, and a great many gleaned from compadres and passengers in the airline business. Those helpful individuals who participated in the collection and recollection process were invariably willing to research "their files" and cough up some jewels. Admittedly.. some aren't terribly funny—some are rather sad, in a way, but they do give you a look at how life in the flying game has been lived.

May you enjoy this collection of short articles and anecdotes, stories that for the most part will make you snicker.

Most are God-honest truth; a few may have the ring of a story teller's imagination, and there are lines here and there that are simply opinions (which some of the author's contemporaries may quickly reject.)

For the benefit of those who only occasionally venture skyward via the modern airliner, the tales are written for your understanding. To the aviation-oriented, the author's apologies for the wordiness.

My heartfelt thanks go out to all the many contributors who gave of their time and memories. That goes double for the voluntary (well, mostly..) effort of editors Ron R. Jensen and Patrick A. Thiele. Enough can't be said for the hand behind the throttle on this word processor. Wives can do a lot for a man's progress, and my Anna has kept her cool; picking up the slack around the homestead while the "help" was doodling through life with a capricious computer.

R. T.

INTRODUCTION

Nothing has captivated so many people as the advancements made in aviation. In great leaps and bounds throughout the 20th century, humans by the score; by the hundreds; by the thousands; now by the millions, have risen skyward to experience man's ageless dream: To be airborne.

Within this century World War I fighter aces were seen as glamorous daredevils who followed the likes of Wilbur and Orville Wright. Charles Lindbergh's dramatic solo flight across the Atlantic focused young men's attention on aviation; Amelia Earhart did much the same for the female sex. In the 1930's school children only half a decade from their maturation saw the challenges in aerial flight.

They couldn't resist. No nation in the civilized world was exempt.

It was an era of bold experimentation by the youthful which frequently appeared to defy Mother Nature and gravity; often frightening the youngsters' parents. The occasional failures only helped to stimulate pilots and challenge would-be pilots to become more knowledgeable; the aircraft industry to make greater advances. It was an overall effort that provided impetus to the world's gigantic aerial accomplishments of World War II.

The result was a massive use of air power for both logistics support and offensive operations. The military's success greatly expedited the public's postwar ventures into an expanded environment. Commercial air transportation began zooming into an era of speed and distance, outperforming the great liners of the oceans and the wheels of rail and road.

Air became more than a passive part of our life. For today we have a worldwide network of skyways that has blossomed into an unlimited number of routes that are routinely available to millions of passengers.

Therefore, to be up in the air is a frequent human condition. And to be very human—and American—about flight is to laugh, to love, to be at ease, to joke, and yes, at times most unwelcome.. to make mistakes.

The book's title, "To AIR is Human" is, of course, a play on words; a definite, misspelled takeoff on the old phrase which expects all humans will make occasional errors.

But the author's interest really lay in collecting examples of life on a happy note. To wit;.. (literally).. So the book is mostly about humor.. laughs, or even just a smile. Your choice.

Yet, there is more. Anthologies on separate phases of aviation; a bit of education on the subject; how it began for the author, and how it ended in tragedy for a fellow pilot or two.

The project has been a long, almost never-ending one.. Some stories are even older(!) than the writer. It is regrettable the book doesn't include more viewpoints and comments from folks who occupied the passenger seats; people who, if they fly often, undoubtedly have stories upon stories.

In years past (thirty and beyond) pranks and practical jokes were just as common in the airline world as anywhere else. Yet only a very few have come close to jeopardizing the total safety of a flight, and to be brutally honest, some of the perpetrators of the time were terribly guilty of what is today called "sexual harassment."

You will find certain stories here where use of names could result in unwarranted embarrassment to either an individual or to an airline. Leaving such identification out of the book should not detract from your pleasure.

Of course times have changed. Today's world of flight is not conducive to pranks aboard a flying vehicle. Things we did over thirty or more years ago may have been tolerated and quietly ignored by officialdom then.

Not so true today. Of necessity the regulated environment and precision safety of today's aviation world limits the gags and pranks to places other than aboard the airplane. That's not to say humor and some restricted form of fun and games have disappeared, but the author found no evidence to indicate there is any reason to be concerned for safety.

Flying... being the pilot.. was always fun for those who truly loved the business. They were guys and gals who would have done the work for free if economic necessities weren't established facts of life. Especially in the early days before everybody started doing it. The attraction of always being on the edge of danger may have tempted some. We accepted that potential hazard to our health the way most young folks do: "Yeah, it could happen.. I could spin-in to some hay field or bang myself into a cloud with rocks in it.. it could happen, but not likely if I do my job correctly."

The thrill most pilots got out of flying came from skirting danger with a mantle of confidence. Pilots of fighter aircraft are a prime example. (Perhaps it was the same with many of the passengers from an earlier era.) Confidence was necessary because the lack of it tends to open the gates to fear; to insecurity; in essence clouding the mind with doubt, confusion and indecision.

Of course those pilots who "bought the farm" or "boogered in" from some misguided attempt to show off usually had all kinds of confidence, too. Invariably their sad end might well have been from misplaced confidence or trying a maneuver for which they were not properly prepared.

Remember the small boys who were first-time observers of an activity adults or bigger kids were enjoying? Younger kids would always say: "Oh, I can do that." Their initial try: A sloppy failure, but they had a great time showing off.

Like the little kids above, a few pilots simply didn't have the skills or the knowledge to cope with their project of the moment. So certainly... bold confidence was not enough. More was needed. It was all part of what we learned to appreciate as "flight experience." Of knowing the limitations; of calculating the risks.

Commercial airline pilots are hired for their inherent skills and confidence. It takes years of training, however, to enhance their confidence and acquire the special skills an airline and the federal government demand of airliner captains. Much of that is derived from junior pilots riding in the cockpit's "right" seat—sometimes for years—being a copilot to a seasoned pilot who has all of the necessary qualifications that cause the captain to be in the "left" seat—the captain's own.

The air becomes their environment; an arena of sky, clouds, rain, snow and global distance they are dedicated to conquer safely.. smoothly and timely. In their everyday jobs there is always a challenge: to make every flight better than the last.

Every pilot has experienced the thrills that came from being aloft and alone. Even in the cockpit of an airliner that thrill never really disappears. And it certainly doesn't diminish in the worlds of skydiving and soaring. The sky as seen and felt from an altitude far above the earth is a 'high' that must be on a par with what the adventurous individual feels when he or she treks solo through a mountain wilderness, or dives with confidence in the realm of sharks.

Passengers are seldom caught up in the real excitement of abandoning their place on Mother Earth. Yes, they 'oo' and 'ahh' on their initial flight (unless they are the nervous type) but they never quite discover the same feel of freedom as do the pilots.

Understandably, passengers can't be expected to just "let go," but most have learned to rely upon the regulations that have fostered their pilot's qualifications. They can have little more than a "gut feeling" about whether to embark on a given flight. Some inherently worry about one factor or another: how good the pilot is... can the pilot manage in this weather?... the top of the plane's tail is crooked... does the captain know that? That member of the flight crew looks awfully young... etc.

For what it may be worth to all the fearful, your airline captain and the vast majority of pilots who are commercially licensed to fly passengers have absolutely no intention of doing anything that is truly daring. They channel their skill and confidence into flying with a maximum of safety, accuracy and comfort.

Be assured, the pilot is quite conscious of safety. Further, pilots love to make a favorable impression on their precious cargo. Airline pilots tend to do so by making all of their moves as smoothly as possible... if you, as a passenger, can barely feel the action that is occurring, the pilot "done good."

Presumptuous of me to write as though some of you have doubts about the safety of air transportation. The relatively few individuals in that category would be unlikely to have the slightest interest in "To AIR is Human." Unless, of course, you tell 'em how reading this book might help change their viewpoints about the flying game.

But... It's been fun producing it. Hope you enjoy the results.

Almost forgotten by anyone but dedicated aviation history buffs is the story of the Army's (and man's) first airborne crossing of the Pacific Ocean between California and Hawaii. (A Navy seaplane had made a crossing two years earlier, but not all via the air. They landed at sea and sailed over 200 miles before reaching land.)

An Army plane arrived in "pineapple country" on June 29, 1927, under the command of two Army lieutenants. It was an historic undertaking, drawing praise from the Army command and the nation's major newspapers.

The two pilots—Lt. L. J. Maitland and Lt. A. F. Hegenberger—both bore names relatively uncommon in the U. S. and especially so in Hawaii (where they were much idolized by the press and the local populace.) Both went on to further their careers in military aviation past World War II, and both survived to live in retirement.

What is surprising, but reportedly coincidental, is Hegenberger's choice of a retirement locale.

In 1965 he was living in Maitland, Florida.

In the era of the Wright brothers, Glenn Curtiss grew famous by producing the earliest aircraft in "show business." Aviators found an air show would always draw a crowd; used models built by Curtiss. This replica is very much the same as an early predecessor which was the first to be launched from, and landed upon, a naval vessel in 1910-11. In 1912 a daredevil pilot successfully flew a similar Curtiss from the roof of the Multnomah Hotel, Portland, Oregon.

IN THE BEGINNING

In keeping with the title of this book, it is almost obligatory to present stories about Louis Blériot, the fabulous Frenchman, and the equally famous Wright brothers, Wilbur and Orville. All names synonymous with early aviation.

Blériot's life was, like the brothers Wright, one of total dedication and determination. Little Louis, however, always seemed to accomplish his learning curves in a more painful way; efforts filled with mishap after mishap.

Like many men of his time, Blériot initially decided the flight characteristics of birds had to be the way to go. "Who flies with more grace and beauty than a bird?"

His first known venture was a set of wings—wings that emulated as precisely as possible that of a bird. It was a mechanical contraption capable of creating movement, but wings unable to move Blériot's machine, other than to flap itself into rubble.

Blériot built many other devices, the initial machines totally different in their basic design. He was up to eight or nine ideas before he found an aerial attitude we call "flight."

And unlike the brothers Wright, Louis had less patience and somewhat greater interest in gambling. With each of his various new models, he wasted little time before attempting to get airborne. It appeared he developed theories as result of his past tries at flying. History would do Blériot an injustice, however, to imply he had "more guts than brains" or that he failed to consider the value of experimentations of others.

(People in Louis' neighborhood usually became excited about watching the action if they knew Louis was planning to test another flying machine. Nearly everyone of his first nine made for plenty of excitement—reportedly Louis crashed in each. What was surprising, he made it through all of them without killing himself.)

Despite holding what is believed to be the European—and possibly a world—record for the number of crashes an aeronaut could successfully experience, Blériot was undaunted. He finally divined a design format that set the pattern for the future. The fuselage was built like a long box, but it had tail surfaces; wing; engine, and landing gear much like most of the light aircraft we've seen for seventy-five years. By today's standards, of course, it was indeed a flimsy-looking monoplane.

With his eleventh design, he believed he had made it as a builder of aircraft. He took that latest model and accepted the challenge to fly the English Channel. It was a winner. On July 13, 1909, Blériot was the first man in a winged machine to complete that 22 mile flight. Yet, his most successful aircraft never flew again. It became an instant museum piece.

It did, however, net him a handsome prize. Moreover, he fulfilled a plan unlike any of his competitors—establishing a market for his aircraft. In just two days Blériot claimed to have received orders for one hundred of his "aeroplanes."

One such sale was made to a man living in the state of Ohio, U.S.A. The plane had no sooner tried the air in Ohio with its American owner at the helm when it suffered damage in a landing. (Rather like many of Louis' other aircraft.) It was repaired; flew again, and somewhere within a few years it got bunged up and no longer excited its owner. That was that. It wasn't considered airworthy any longer. Eventually some aviation enthusiast bought the now ancient relic and had it shipped west to California. Nothing rather exciting happened until a man named Wardle acquired it in 1967.

Wardle was a restoration expert, a pilot and a mechanic. Most of all he had a love for old aircraft. The Blériot got him wound up!

Within three years he had struggled through weekends and holidays to make his Blériot flyable, for he had acquired the plane in its entirety. It was a challenge he couldn't resist. Rebuilding and flying old Wacos and Bellancas was fun, and they were considered classics, too, but they were twenty years behind the Blériot of 1909!

Wardle didn't intend to rebuild Louis' little jewel to have it sit in a museum. He was putting it together to see it fly.. to fly with himself in the cockpit.

However it quickly became obvious he was dealing with some very ancient parts and pieces. A good portion of which were just not up to what Wardle knew would be safe to fly. In the end he mounted a modern 65 HP engine fitted with a new propeller. There were other changes made that added to the safety factors involving an airplane 61 years old, but little was done to alter the overall appearance of the Blériot. At Santa Paula, California, in 1970, Mr. Shirley Wardle flew the ol' bird for the first time. It was a monumental success.

More than one ancient airplane ended up in a museum, of course, just as do some of the more modern aircraft. The famous Smithsonian Air and Space Museum has a collection that will knock your eyes out! But there are dozens more around the globe, each having a fantastic collection of aircraft and memorabilia.

But the most distinguished aircraft in the world nearly failed to make it into the prestigious Smithsonian—the Wright brothers' *Flyer*. In 1903, the world's first successful powered, piloted aircraft completed its brief flights over the sands near Kill Devil Hill, North Carolina. Yet it came dangerously close to never becoming a museum piece in its current home: The Smithsonian in Washington, D. C.

"Why? Orville and Wilbur Wright were Americans, weren't they?"

Oh, they were very American, but the Wright brothers were so dedicated in their belief about their aviation discoveries, Orville always felt the Smithsonian had continually given the inventive Wright family less credit than he and his deceased brother deserved.

The Wrights conducted an amazing number of rather technical experiments before presenting their accomplishments to the world. A far cry from the actions of other more impulsive would-be aeronauts.

As if weather conditions don't have an effect on our flights in today's world, you can imagine how concerned the Wrights became when rain and snow whistled in from the north for several days just as the *Flyer* was ready to make its initial takeoff. Orville—ever the opportunist to learn more—wrote about making use of the delay:

"...we arranged a mechanism to measure automatically the duration of a flight from the time the machine started to move forward to the time it stopped, the distance traveled through the air in that time and the number of revolutions made by the motor and propeller. A stopwatch took the time, an anemometer measured the air traveled through and a counter took the number of revolutions made by the propellers. The watch, anemometer and revolution counter were all automatically started and stopped simultaneously. From data thus obtained we expected to prove or disprove the accuracy of our propeller calculations."

Wow!.. that sounds complicated to the author nearly 100 years after their outstanding efforts! Remember.. this was all being done without today's magical electronic boxes!.. not to mention a decided lack of proven aerodynamic principles.

The fact the Wright's formal education was limited to years spent in high school did not deter their efforts to gain aeronautical knowledge, the existence of meaningful experiments being largely nil.

Wilbur Wright himself wrote: "After much study we finally concluded that tails were a source of trouble rather than of assistance, and therefore we decided to dispense with them altogether. It seemed reasonable that if the body of the operator (pilot) could be placed in a horizontal position instead of the upright, as in the machines of ..(others).. the wind resistance could be very materially reduced... a full half horsepower could be saved by this change..."

Virtually all of the Wright brothers attention to research and experimentation barely saw the light of day. It was not displayed openly to other budding aeronauts, nor to the members of the press. They believed the powered aircraft had a future, that someday it would become a commercial success. Each of their developments took years to gain even their own approval; the U. S. Patent Office was to take even longer.

Their rather intense secrecy, combined with the more obvious scientific explorations of Otto Lilienthal and Octave Chanute, made it easy for the famed Smithsonian Museum to give little credit to the Wright brothers. The museum's doubt was aided by the fact their own Secretary of the institution, Samuel P. Langley, a distinguished scientist, had been just as active in aeronautical endeavors as had Chanute and Lilienthal. As the Wrights were in the Carolina's conducting their tests, Langley did, in fact, develop a design that later made sense to engineers. However, unlike his smaller scale models, it was unsound structurally and there appeared to be no definitive plan for steering, or controlling the craft. The would-be pilot apparently had no concept of how to perform his necessary function and both of Langley's excellent full-size models crashed on takeoff.

The result of the Smithsonian's apparent reluctance to shed more light on the Wright's rather unflamboyant accomplishments caused a feud between Orville and the museum following Wilbur's death. It took Orville Wright thirty years to "forgive" the museum. In 1928 he literally "gave" the famous first machine to the Science Museum, London, England, until such time as he might like the plane returned. That dispute lasted until 1942, at which time Orville finally agreed the Smithsonian Institute could take custody of the *Flyer*.

Timing for the *Flyer's* transfer couldn't have been worse. A lengthy war was at its zenith, London being heavily bombed day and night. A highly impractical time to move the plane back to the U. S.

While the end of the oppressive war occurred in 1945, the actual transfer of the airplane did not come about until 1948, the same year Orville Wright's spirit flew to a more heavenly realm.

And there's a humorous sidebar story relating to the planned transfer of the *Flyer*. An executive of the world-class airline of the era—PanAm—told the English museum's curator they'd be happy and honored to fly the famous "first" aircraft back to the U. S. Meaning, of course, to air freight Wright's original in one of PanAm's aircraft.

The surprised curator, not exactly an aeronautics expert, thought the PanAm representative meant a PanAm pilot would be assigned to help the old bird wing its way over the wide Atlantic.

The curator did at least know the size of the *Flyer*'s fuel tank, however, and to the Pan Am rep, volunteered something to the effect "it's terribly decent of you, but do you think you should chance it? The bloody old plane has absolutely no range."

With the thought of traveling a short distance by air, there is the story about a rare and early aviator in Hawaii.

In 1929 when civilian airplanes were also a rarity in Hawaii, the projected start of an airline between the islands had become a "hot" topic at many service club meetings.

A man who was present at one such gathering was Hawaii's oldest aviator, Mr. E. H. Lewis.

The group had somehow taken to "roasting" Lewis. The editor of the Honolulu Star-Bulletin drew some chuckles by telling those present about Lewis' first involvement in aerial navigation—when Lewis was thrown from the back of a polo pony.

Recognizable to aviation enthusiasts is the forerunner to Lindbergh's "Spirit of St. Louis." Ryan Aircraft, a small company in California, produced the Spirit from this basic, but smaller design, in 60 working days. Price for Lindy's special plane, including engine, came to $10,500.

LEARNING WHILE YEARNING

Memories of a pilot's beginning days involve a touch of excitement, humbleness and embarrassment. And there are dozens of stories that match the action in the lives of all persons who are dedicated aerial enthusiasts.

In 1940, the United States foresaw its entry into World War II and perceived the need for pilots. The Civil Pilot Training program was born, a program where young people—mostly males—were given the chance to earn their private pilot's license, at government expense.

As a teenaged student the author enrolled. With 15 others he was assigned to learn flying in a 65-horsepower Aeronca Chief, a trusty two-seater monoplane which was always a personal disappointment for one important reason:

Its cockpit didn't have a stick.. a control stick like *"real"* airplanes are always supposed to have." The Chief had a "steering wheel." Not just one, but two. For those of us brought up to believe every airplane had to have a "joystick," the aircraft was a decided letdown.

The battle aces of World War One always flew their Spads, Nieuports, and Sopwiths with a stick... Ol' Charlie Lindbergh struggled for 33 hours across the Atlantic using a stick. Any other method just didn't make sense and it was a dead certainty no Navy pilot ever used a steering wheel when he flew off an aircraft carrier. (Subconsciously it was feared this issue might affect a young man's future career as a naval aviator!)

After "studying" flying during all those adolescent years, if anyone had the audacity to suggest a flying career could begin in a plane with a "steering wheel" instead of a joystick, we flight oriented "know-it-alls" would have laughed that individual out of the room.

Early flights in the steering wheeled-Chief were filled with complaints from instructor Bob Phelps. His latest junior birdman was always trying to make turns by turning the "wheel" instead of using those things on the cockpit floor—the rudder pedals.

During those first attempts at flight, even getting the Chief to roll straight down the runway was a major problem. On takeoff the Aeronca would invariably start veering to the left. The torque from an engine at full power caused that—certainly not the pilot, but it was his job to correct the problem. How? By using the rudder pedals. Phelps' slow-learning student would attempt to stop such movement by turning the "steering wheel" to the right. It never worked.

"DON'T keep using the wheel," Phelps would say. "All the control wheel does is move the ailerons out there," he said pointing at the plane's wingtips. "Use the rudder pedals... the rudder is what changes the plane's direction, not the wheel."

It took nearly 20 hours of flight time in the Chief before Phelps' latest "hot-shot" would accept the concept.

Sometime later in the training program, one of the two young ladies out on a solo practice flight failed to return to the airport on schedule. But prior to the initiation of a search, Miss Caroline was on the phone to the boss flight instructor, Jim Dewey.

Caroline was obviously in some kind of trouble and apparently near the point of panic.

These were her very words:

"Mr. Dewey, I made a forced landing." Nothing more, just: "I made a forced landing." Before poor Jim Dewey could begin to ask *WHERE* she made the landing, she hung up.

Fortunately for Jim and his staff, the flight training area covered only a few square miles. The local terrain consisted of more bean fields than orchards, so an emergency landing in that part of the county was a "piece of cake."

"Even a girl could do it." And she did. Very successfully.

To the fledgling flier any airport with a half dozen aircraft is an exciting place.

And in 1940 Oxnard, California, had excitement.

One fascinating airplane was the super slick, single-engine Beechcraft with a cabin that could carry 4 or 5 people. The fanciest biplane in the nation was called a "staggerwing" because the upper wing was set further aft across the body of the airplane than was the lower wing. (An unusual creation eventually becoming a classic, though the concept never caught on with other builders of flying machines.) It was, however, the most modern private aircraft of its time, with retractable landing gear and a "huge" 225 horsepower radial engine, it looked as though it could fly as fast as 200 miles per hour. Not that any of us got an opportunity to find out. None of us were ever even offered a ride in it.

That undeniably, outstandingly beautiful, shiny, sleek machine belonged to a wealthy bachelor lady, a spinster, if you will... rather elderly.. well, as old as any of our mothers.

She lived up the coast near Santa Barbara, and for reasons of her own, kept the airplane 35 miles away in the Oxnard hangar. The plane's only pilot was the lady herself. The trips she took were infrequent, but ofttimes to distant points within the western part of the nation; one into central America. She was far ahead of her time.

This spinster lady was never openly criticized by our class of students... (we weren't smart enough about aviation to be criticizing anyone with a license.) Even our two instructors kept their tongues, though it gradually became rather obvious the lady's aviation talent and headwork could use some help. While she was a pleasant, friendly sort; she rarely demonstrated a sense of awareness. (Every time she fired up the Beechcraft and moved out of her parking spot, she'd blow a cloud of dust into the hangar, an event that never endeared her to the mechanics.)

After one of her journeys into the southwest, she returned with her staggerwing intact. (The plane was notorious for its characteristic of whirling around in a maddening circle [a "groundloop"] during takeoffs and landings while under the inept guidance of a novice.) She arrived with her camera completely out of film and with the report she had flown into and over the Grand Canyon.

She offered us a chance to view the first color movies of the fabulous natural wonder of the western world. She had flown the plane and reportedly shot the film, as well. As student fliers we were an appreciative audience. Our instructors enjoyed the film, also, but were almost flabbergasted to see much of her camera work had been done while she was flying *below* the rim of the canyon. One instructor politely questioned the lady on that fact once the film had run its course.

"What would you have done if the engine quit?"

"Well," she answered in a manner that made hers the only logical one, "it just couldn't quit. There was no place to *land!*"

Then there was the arrival of the movie star, the late actor Robert Taylor. Like us, he had become enamored of flying. One bright morning he and his instructor breezed into Oxnard for a coffee break.

To us would-be aviators, the aircraft in which he arrived was almost as captivating as being in the presence of the well-known screen actor himself.

Taylor must have believed learning to fly was enhanced by flying in something better and fancier than the plane like the Aeronca or the one which coincidentally bore his last name: The Taylorcraft. Bob Taylor had his very own—and very new—Fairchild 24, a four-place high-wing monoplane; one that fairly sparkled in shiny black paint trimmed stylishly in an intense yellow. Now, *there* was an airplane!

We all had our opportunities to speak with him, asking him any number of questions, most of them about his airplane and his flying. Some of us came away a bit smug after Mr. Taylor and his instructor had departed.

Bob Taylor may have had his own personal instructor and his very own shiny new Fairchild, but our talks with him had revealed the fact he had flown 12 hours but had yet to fly solo.

Most of us made our initial solo flight after only six hours of instruction. Obviously we believed this made us "super-brilliant" fliers.

None of us seemed to realize what Jim Dewey considered pertinent: "If you had Robert Taylor's money and his airplane, wouldn't you like to just fly here and there to show off?"

The spring and summer of 1940 had filled thirty of us junior college kids with the real spirit of aviation. Since we all achieved the coveted pilot's license, it obviously could be assumed that we were "something special"... that the government, in all its wisdom, had certainly picked the right place to find pilots.

But now those of us having the desire to exercise our legal right to fly, and were too young to join any of the country's aviation ranks, were forced to BUY our flight time. When the cost of renting a plane came to a whopping $4 per hour for even the cheapest, my 37 cents an hour pay at the local gas station made it a hard choice. Shrewd thinking and good planning had to be developed.

Girls or airplanes. Just how important were either? When you have a burning desire to become a flying ace, yet exist on a meager income, you give up chasing after skirts.

Well... more or less. Sometimes you took a lady flying—even if you had to borrow the money! Unfortunately, the financial responsibility all fell on the great aviator's thin wallet.

And sister Joyce was the only family member who dared leave the ground in an airplane. Oh sure... the others trusted "their pilot," they just didn't think flying was safe. The upshot of it all, they were willing to let Joyce zoom off the planet on a potentially fateful mission, but they damned sure weren't going to finance such a venture.

The end result, since Joyce was only 13 and without an income capable of supporting the rental of airplanes, big brother had to care for *that* problem, as well. But she was ready.

And she received the "cheap treatment"—the $4 per hour, 40-horsepower Piper Cub.

Flying with her daring sibling proved to be a one-time deal. Probably because Joyce's feet got wet.

"Her feet got wet??"

It went this way...

Pilot and passenger hustled to the airport, ready to board their bright-yellow flying machine. Following the demonstration of skill in making a successful takeoff, the flight became action-filled. Such as watching the speed-limited autos below gradually outdistance our airborne steed. (Our speed over the ground was less than 40 mph when we flew into a 20 mph wind!)

But soon the joyride was to end. However, by then the wind at the airport had changed direction. It no longer pointed down the length of the runway. It was introducing what was still a problem to a novice pilot: Landing in a crosswind. The subject *may* have been discussed or demonstrated at some earlier time, but only in a plane with brakes.

And the $4 an hour aircraft didn't have brakes.

In any case, for a plane so ill-equipped, a strong crosswind put a demand on the pilot. Both the plane and the wind were ready to match wits with the aeronaut, and if he came half prepared.. well, watch out!

When we landed, we did so using this pilot's standard technique—the engine throttled back until the propeller barely turned. As the brakeless airplane slowed to a crawl, the airplane and the wind jointly made a decision for the pilot.

"Forget the runway," the wind seemed to imply, "let me guide you where I will." The aircraft accepted the challenge. It weathercocked into the wind and turned sharply to the right, departing the runway, promptly stopping in a large, but shallow pool of rainwater.

(In a stiff crosswind, an alert pilot using engine power to blow propwash smartly over the plane's rudder could have easily controlled the crosswind. Brakes or no brakes, the plane would have been steerable by using the rudder.. just as it will steer the aircraft in the air.)

But once in the water, a problem existed—how we were to escape from the embarrassing predicament. There was no help in sight; the hangar area over a half-mile away... *we* were the 'rescue squad.'

We dared not shut down the engine. It had no magic button for starting it again. We should push the aircraft all the way to the hangar??.. No way! Getting our feet wet was the easiest solution. We would push the plane back onto the runway; (carefully avoiding the whirling propeller) taxi back to the flight line and park the aircraft in a nonchalant manner.

The small passenger and her great aviator splashed through the muddy pond; commenced pushing on the horizontal tail surfaces and found our way ashore. We did all the things above, and couldn't have been more nonchalant.

No one ever asked why the yellow Cub's cabin floor got so wet on such a nice day.

Within weeks (after the shoes had dried) sister Joyce's pilot had found a new opportunity: flying in an acrobatic aircraft. The Civil Pilot Training program had been extended to offer a secondary course in larger airplanes with greater power and maneuverability. Other young men had earlier been granted a chance to get into "real" flying, but no one came around begging me to be one of them.

One student who initially made the program dropped out. It left an opening and no one challenged me for it. My designated aircraft would be the very classy Ryan STA, an all-metal bird with an inverted 125 HP liquid-cooled engine.

Almost immediately after takeoff on the first instructional flight, I was pretty sure why the plane's engine was categorized as "inverted".. the aircraft seemed to fly that way during a great portion of every flight!

Never will I forget our first takeoff. We weren't 1500 feet in the air when the instructor pilot introduced me to aerobatics.. all at the speed of light (or so it seemed then.) He later told me it was a snaproll.

I believed the part about the snap, but was hard pressed to describe *what* the hell we did.

But aerobatics *was* the program. I got so I could do a snap-roll in my sleep. I learned to do many things my heart and my brain accepted; unfortunately my stomach rejected both the whirling activity and many of my breakfasts. Having "tossed my cookies" 4 times in only 8 hours of flight, the flying school boss suggested there was a good probability I wasn't cut out to be a pilot.

We didn't altogether agree on that point, but I had taken a dislike to the embarrassment of having to scrub down the side of the Ryan every other time I had been airborne. Which brings up a sidebar story involving myself, the messed up Ryan and an idle, elderly observer, a man who obviously didn't know too much about airplanes, but one certainly interested in learning.

This fellow watched me washing down the right side of the Ryan. Watched me all of half an hour, then finally asked:

"Has thet there machine got a RE-verse in it?"

I had half a notion to tell him: "No, we took it out," but thought better of being a smart-ass, realizing such a response wouldn't have helped his education much.

But that was my last day in the program. The Ryan was a beautiful bird and the instructor was a great fellow, but the three of us just didn't get along.

Anyhow, the Navy was already calling my group of non-flying reservists into active service. It was extremely distanced from aviation, but as soon as my age met the Naval Aviation pilot requirements, I would quickly sign up.

After a year's wait, that moment came to pass. I was accepted. The CPT program had seemed exciting, but it didn't hold a candle to Navy training.

Trainee Navy pilots began their careers in the sturdy yellow biplanes lovingly referred to as "yellow perils." Each plane carried two people, one was the instructor; the other a "barely intelligent being."

Cadet training periods were usually conducted with one's "flight," which didn't necessarily mean anyone was airborne, it was used in lieu of the civilian word 'group.' But when cadets did get to fly, as many as 26-30 in a like number of airplanes would leap up (some planes with instructors aboard; some without.)

The majority of yellow peril flying was not done from a conventional airport with runways and taxiways. A huge asphalt mat was the site of all departures and landings. Wind direction being important to such activity, the large circular mat provided an unlimited number of potential directions.

At this one base, entry into the left-circling traffic pattern was always made from the northeast. The control tower, located on the west side of the mat, chose the direction of takeoffs and landings for everybody.

But since radios were not in vogue for primary trainer-type airplanes, tower controllers led aircraft into the takeoff direction by hanging a series of large, brightly colored balls high above the tower. One orange ball meant north, for example; two, another direction; a series of yellow balls meant still another direction, etc. Mounted far out at the edge of the field was a three-dimensional contraption that landing aircraft could easily see from the air. It was manually pointed in the direction the Navy wanted us to land. When the balls were changed above the tower, a responsible individual was to adjust the position of the 3-D contraption as well. Each pilot, whether coming or going, had the obligation to check one of the indicators before takeoff or landing.

The tower personnel were expected to make any changes to the traffic flow BEFORE the next arrival time of the abundant yellow perils, many of whom would be landing almost simultaneously across the broad expanse of the mat.

A sudden windshift could put the tower people on the spot should a change occur when the next flight of yellow birds was entering the traffic pattern for landing.

And one day that situation occurred. The wind shifted as planes started returning. Pilots of the first six planes looked at the 3-D gadget which clearly implied: "Land to the west." It required they fly an almost full circle of the field.

As the flight of six approached the tower, (its personnel had quickly begun changing the colored balls) the wind was no longer blowing from the west. It had shifted 180 degrees and landings should be made *toward* the east, not from it! As the first flight of aircraft passed the tower, none of that group observed the new information, and in their minds the "correct" direction for landing had been provided by the 3-D tetrahedron. Toward the *west!*

Then the 3-D wind director down near the landing mat was changed—just in time for the next group of planes to clearly read their landing direction should be made toward the east.

By then the initial six planes had nearly completed their circle and were no longer interested in looking at wind indicators. They knew in which direction they were going to land: West. They began their descent, making their final turn onto a westerly heading for landing.. wing-tip to wing-tip.

Already in the pattern north of the field, the leader of the second incoming group of five looked at the newly changed 3-D gadget and accepted the request to "land east." Like sheep, everyone else followed the leader, each student solo flier no doubt less concerned about wind than a possibility of collision with an adjacent aircraft. In making their turn to the east for the final landing approach, they also began their descent. Like the first group, all virtually wing-tip to wing-tip.

Each plane in the two groups had dropped down to their last quarter mile of approach; their last leg to a landing.. six side by side coming down from the east; five practically side by side from the west.

Most of the pilots—whether they were solo students or instructors—were so intensely concentrating upon their own landings they never spotted the oncoming aircraft until reaching the point of touchdown. For most it was even later. Two, who must have been sharp, keen-eyed instructors, opened the throttle and climbed away, struggling mightily to rise above the anticipated carnage. During their final approach, none of the pilots in the first flight had seen a red light flashing from the tower.

As the gods would have it, none of the planes collided.

And few could believe nine aircraft, meshing like tines from a pair of forks, could actually land almost simultaneously without incident!

One of the primary areas where the Navy tried to make improved pilots out of well-intended young men was a spanking new air facility at Corpus Christi, Texas. Corpus, as we called it, had a ring of satellite airfields. Each took on some phase of the total pilot training program. One of those air bases was Rodd Field.

A Rodd Field specialty in the general pilot training was night flying for those students still in the beginning stages of flying. That phase was done in a near replica of the Stearman "yellow peril"—a Navy-built standby—officially called the N3N. And, like its newer counterpart, the Stearman biplane, it, too, was painted yellow.

During the author's night for solo flight, the weather was perfect. So clear you could darned near see the lights of a town fifty miles inland.

An instructor, with whom this writer had never flown before, had apparently accepted my relaxed attitude as a sign of confidence; like I must have done it all before and didn't need babysitting. Perhaps he believed he was being misused or pushing his luck to fly cadets at night, rather than being "in the fleet" fighting off kamikazi attacks. In any case, he had no plans to martyr his life with me. He flew one trip around the field and then told me to go ahead without him.

"Do a good job, kid. I'll see ya'."

So, as he sent me out on my own, it was nice to be trusted with my very own airplane, even if I was too ill-trained to realize what I was getting into.

And at first I thought I could handle it with no strain. Only five other cadet buddies of mine were scheduled for that night. Since it was a beautifully clear night, what could go wrong?

I'd done some night flying before. (Big deal!) On a civilian cross-country solo flight from Oxnard, California, to San Fernando Valley and back. Fifty five miles each way. My experience from those days came from getting slightly lost near dusk. I didn't get back to the Oxnard airport until 15 minutes after dark. And in that 15 minutes I couldn't remember how to turn on the red and green navigation lights every flier is supposed to use when flying in darkness.

But at Rodd Field, we big-time fliers, all on our own, in the blackness the war imposed upon coastal areas, were sent up to create a circle around the airfield, each circle intended to generate a landing.

The services referred to our mission as doing "touch-and-goes." They were nothing more than practice landings, and once you made one, you opened the throttle and did your best to get airborne again and rejoin the circle.

One thing I forgot to mention.. in our touch-and-go pattern that night, there were at least four other N3N's. I'd seen their pilots near the schedule board; all from Mexico on an assignment to the U.S. for flight training. So, in reality we had ten planes in our joyful little circle.

It wasn't the easiest thing we ever did. N3N's didn't come equipped with landing lights, and since the Navy was training us for war, none of us, they said, "had any need for lights. Competent night fliers don't use any lights. You learn to land in the dark without them."

Really, it was kind of a Catch-22 deal. To become a *good* night flier, one had to practice. And if one couldn't see the landing field, how could you practice any landings? We were about to find out.

We did have three navigation lights. A white one for a tail light, a red one on the left wingtip, and a green one on the right wing. Every airplane has those as the minimum standard. Just bright enough to be seen by planes having sharp-eyed pilots. (Without them, it would have been absolute mayhem in a great part of the Texas skies during World War II.)

Being an observant young aviator, I could see the good weather had brought out airplanes from most every field affiliated with Corpus Christi, for there was a large number of flickering red and green lights in any direction.

Before the flight began, and the disappearing instructor ran out on me, we were all told: "Stay in the circling pattern and don't wander off." All one had to do, "was follow those white lights up ahead... watch them land and keep your distance.. don't crowd the guy ahead of you."

I think my guide told me how many solo landings I should make and maybe some other sensible things I should do. As it turned out, I didn't remember any of the latter, because pretty soon we had a major problem.

If there were any problems, it was impossible to communicate to or from N3N's. They had no radios, so the tower's only manner of helping would be through use of the standard signal lights; green for takeoff and landing; red for stay where you are—don't takeoff or don't land. On top of the tower was a whirligig green light "meaning the field was open for business"

Suddenly, that light on top of the tower turned red. That meant no landings; no takeoffs. Those of us not actually making an approach or beginning one had no idea what was happening. We had no choice but to keep tooling around our pattern, one after another, until we got in the landing approach position for our final descent to the big hunk of asphalt below.

Once we arrived back over the huge landing mat, each of us could see what our problem was. It was clearly floodlighted below.

An N3N together with its noble pilot had made their final arrival.

The plane was obviously crunched, like it had spun straight down from as much as 300'. It all happened right in the middle of the landing area.

Why? I didn't know, but the incident reminded me of one important factor: a pilot in an airplane without sufficient flying speed when 50-300 feet above the ground is a goner. Better I peek at my own airspeed and also keep watching for the white tail lights of the cadets ahead of me.

Each of us, distraught in various ways, kept up our circle around the field and in less than ten minutes a bright searchlight from high up in the base complex lit up an area in the flat brush country just outside the perimeter fence. Quickly it targeted another heap of yellow fabric that only minutes earlier had been an N3N flying our circle.

Two in one night?? I could hardly believe it! The first one had made me nervous. In fact, it was probably closer to panic.

To make it worse, I had lost sight of both the white lights I was sure belonged to the other N3N's just ahead of me. I was certain neither had gone down for I had followed them through our aborted landing attempt when we initially became aware of the first crashed airplane.

My eyes were instantly three times as alert, as if I had taken a shot of adrenalin. There were aircraft lights all over the sky! The utterly clear sky had brought them all into focus... surely some were as much as 15 miles away; others probably less than two. But any white lights I saw were well off to the west and northwest, completely out of our circle.

My failure to find all of the circling traffic I knew existed told me to get the hell out of the pattern.. to stretch it out, hoping to keep out of the way of other pilots who might have felt the same anxiety I did. My mind was working overtime, telling me it might take some time before the field was cleared of wreckage. If it was being cleared, I'd be happy to let the rest of our N3N's go in first. When I was satisfied the air was reasonably free of competition, *then* I'd go in.

It was about that time I saw two wingtip lights coming.. turning right into me. One red light, one green.. total blackness in between. It's gotta be another plane!!.. *He's coming right at me!.. those two lights getting farther and farther apart!! I kicked right rudder; bent the stick right. A turn wasn't making it!. the lights kept widening; the damned plane was still coming right at me!! Couldn't the dumb SOB see me?? Oh Gawd! No more time.. this is it!*

I was resigned to my fate...I hadn't even had time to think about bailing out.

But nothing happened.. and the lights kept getting farther apart. Finally, the dawn of civilization had nothing on the light that popped on in my brain.

I had been watching the wing lights of two separate aircraft, each probably five or six miles away, but the relative motion of the lights occurred in such a way I was dead certain it was a single airplane turning directly into my path and heading straight for me.

When the stress-filled moments of wondering who had "bought the farm" down below were added to the brief seconds of "real" terror brought on by what I thought was my first "mid-air," I realized the crash of the two planes had to be what caused my vision of sure death. My system was so shook up over the night's crashes I was close to hallucinating, never realizing the imaginary plane that had been so real had a green light on the LEFT wingtip and red on the right. To have been just one approaching aircraft, the left wingtip would have been tipped with a RED light, not a green one.

Scared??..You bet I was scared.. right out of my shorts!

But the night wasn't over. I still had to get back to the home base; to hope my senses were much more relaxed by the time I arrived. I was the last aircraft to land. All others were accounted for.

But there was sadness about the night. Two of the Mexican pilots, one following the other, had approached the field for landing. The first made his touch-and-go landing; the second had been so close he had been waved-off by the attentive runway watch officer.

The result: The pilot completing his momentary landing pushed his throttle forward, left the mat, and climbed straight out and up into the flight path of his buddy who had overtaken him. One pilot went down on the field; the other struggled for a minute or two but failed to keep his plane in the air. Both pilots were killed.

No... there isn't a thing humorous about the last part of the story in this chapter. Such a catastrophe was, and is, an unfortunate part of our existence, but on the occasion of the deaths of those two gentlemen, there were several lessons available to me which were very much a part of the learning experience.

Baron von Richthofen made his mark as an "ace" in World War I by flying in one of Anthony Fokker's famous triplanes, much like this replica flown in the U. S.

75 years makes a world of difference!

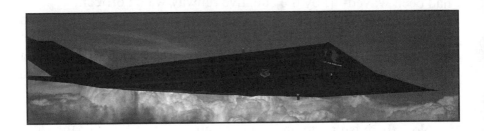

Hidden behind a veil of secrecy; flown only at night from an isolated Air Force base, and painted solid black, the U. S. built "stealth" F-117 fighter allegedly evaded both radar and the public until the Gulf War in 1991. Some unofficial reports indicate its unusual design, and its creation from composite materials, have succeeded in hampering most of radar's penetrating scan.

IN DAYS OF YORE.. THE DC-3

Story tellers digging into the intriguing "old days" talk and write about anything or anybody of historical note, inviting us to appreciate those echoes of the past, to reignite fires of memory.

Is the world of aviation any different? Not in the least.

Flying, past and present, is filled with stories. We could relate dozens of tales about fliers and their phenomenal experiences, so it's only natural we remember to deal with at least one of the all-time great airplanes.

We've chosen one, but many aircraft invariably captivated the heart of the people who built, flew or fixed them. The planes of World War II, for example, fostered really honest-to-God respect by man for machine. And some fellows were willing to believe the fondness was reciprocated. Even though the airplanes were frequently abused by their pilots, or "shot up" by the enemy, the strength of the airframe and the stamina of the engines saved many an aviator's neck. The result was a long lasting love affair.

One aircraft that deserves the all-time merit award is the Douglas DC-3. A noncombatant by design, it had a phenomenal record during World War II and has been working at different jobs in all the years since. It's a plane that probably gets little respect from the public of today, but is still held in high esteem by the people who manned and supported it. Experienced aircraft veterans call the DC-3 Mr. Douglas' finest product, and look upon the plane as the "champion of the airways." In peacetime or wartime, it did what it was supposed to do: Fly safely. Just do your thing, baby! No fancy stuff and no flapping along so high above the clouds a passenger couldn't view the creative wonders of the world below.

Maybe the DC-3 "ain't no big deal," but it's just a shame an unknowing public and the youngsters in aviation give little if any thought to the successes of an aircraft that has become the most durable and dependable bird in the world. Because of those very features, the airplane was commonly taken for granted.

It is a classic passenger and cargo carrying airplane first built in the mid-1930's and many are still alive and well worldwide. The DC-3 was so successful as a relatively newborn infant it was the chosen equipment for 90% of America's airways by 1939. It started its career with surprisingly few inherent technical defects. It kept on flying when sections of wings and other parts had been severely damaged. While the DC-3 began life as the aerial vehicle that put safety and financial success into the airline world, its war record is no small listing on the pages of history, either.

With the outbreak of World War II, this "civilian" jumped in with both engines turning. The military versions, which bore the Army designation C-47, and R4D when it took on a Navy look, commonly were all called a "gooney bird." It flew by the thousands. By 1948 (when production stopped) nearly 11,000 had been built; most of them for the armed services. When it comes to sharing in wartime responsibilities, the ol' bird supported every major military engagement in the 20th century except World War I. That means one thing: It has been around for 60 years!

It was designed for a maximum of 21 passengers, yet known to have flown 93 on an emergency basis. Been the recipient of an in-flight bomb explosion that destroyed one fuel tank and part of the fuselage, yet landed safely. The horror tales are endless.

It had great success as an aircraft capable of surviving horrendous weather conditions, yet the cockpit leaked so much water pilots fondly commented about "light rain showers outside; heavy showers inside." So it wasn't air tight!.. so the cabin wasn't terribly warm in freezing weather or politely air-conditioned and pressurized in the summer!.. so it didn't have jet engines and was pulled through the air with those windy propellers! So what? It had the heart of a hero.

The DC-3 invariably got passengers to and from their destinations. Not with aplomb, perhaps; maybe not even on time. Still.. it was always kinda fun. At least for some of us lucky enough to be associated with the "3."

Retired United captain Charlie Barnard recalls an incident in his first year as pilot in command. Like so many of the stories in this book, it involved the venerable DC-3, but in 1946 that airplane was just about the best the airlines had to offer.

And Charlie could have used more. More altitude; more power, more dry, warm air. For various reasons none of those more desirable items were available. It was November in the midwest.

En route to Denver, just west of Omaha, he was deep in the clouds; unbelievably deep in ice. Ice on the wings; on the propellers; on the windshield; on the engine air scoops to the carburetors.. ice everywhere! Repeatedly, he kept radio calls going into the company communications system, asking them to phone Air Traffic Control for a change in altitude—anything to get out of the severe icing that was burdening the overworked DC-3. The answer was always: "Unable."

From weather reports, Charlie learned all airfields along his route were unusable—"below minimums" is the term. Only Denver and Pueblo still had acceptable weather.

Meanwhile, there were fingers of ice off of the leading edges of any aircraft surface. The windshield finally froze over. The big deicer boots periodically pulsated along the forward edge of the wings, barely cracking the ice, and the long fingers—huge streamlined needles of ice—grew ever longer. Ice forming on the propellers was cleared by brief, sudden increases in propeller speed, flailing the ice loudly against the sides of the aircraft.

As the ice became thicker and heavier, Charlie kept adding power until he finally reached the point where the engines were providing maximum continuous power.

Now even the cockpit's side windows had iced over; despite the massive output of engine power the besieged aircraft struggled to fly at an indicated airspeed of only 90 miles per hour, barely adequate flying speed! What was worse, the rudder began to swing, slowly full left, then slowly full right.. a strange and unusual phenomena.

But the sturdy DC-3 kept slugging ahead and shortly before reaching Denver, Charlie was able to create a small clear space on his windshield. At least no further icing was occurring, but he was still faced with an overburden of ice on much of the airplane's wing and tail surfaces.

Then the clouds began to break and Charlie could actually see the airport. He felt blessed he would have the opportunity to fly a visual approach into Denver, for he had been deeply concerned about having to approach the field while in the clouds. If that had been necessary, the required turns, if made "by the book," would aggravate the overloaded wings; logically create a stall and send the straining aircraft into the ground. Already Charlie had attempted a shallow turn to the left, testing the DC-3 for its willingness to fly while maneuvering under the weight and disruption of air flow across the wings. In reaching a slight 10 degrees of bank, Charlie found the plane commencing to shudder and shake.. the first indications of a dangerous and fatal loss of flying speed.

In the end, Charlie cautiously used only a 5 degree bank of the wings as he turned into his landing approach. Then deliberately kept his landing gear in the up position until the very last moment to avoid "drag" or obstruction to the airflow that was barely supporting the plane's flight.

Charlie's trip was one of the last to make it into Denver on that day. After he landed, a mechanic entered the cockpit overwhelmed by the amount of ice Charlie had brought into town.

"Kee-ryst!" he exclaimed, "I've never seen such ice on an airplane before!"

The storm kept Denver shutdown for several days, and ever after, Captain Barnard tactfully chose to avoid ice anytime he could.

"I'll drink to that.. Uhh, no ice, please."

Captain Paul White has a story about flying this famous aircraft in the 1960's some years after long-range jets had been carrying passengers from one big airport to another. His DC-3 was scheduled to fly passengers from the "big" airport to a small one 120 miles away.

After Paul had landed at this little "down country" airport and was leaving the cockpit, he spots this pleasant, grandmotherly-type lady still seated in a window seat just over the airplane's wing.

"Young man," she says, "you're the captain, are you?"

And Paul, being the pleasant fellow he is, smiles and admitted she had the right man.

"Well, I have a question for you, Captain." Then, she points out a window and asks: "What are those dooley-whoppers out there?"

Dooley-whoppers? Then Paul realizes this elderly lady must have been a beginner at the flying business. Obviously she had ridden to the "big" airport in one of the large jet airliners and it was quite probable she had never before ridden in any aircraft. Because Paul had figured out what she meant, he patiently explained what dooley-whoppers really were: Propellers.

From that story you can readily see how education can better your life. Even if it isn't too apparent, it brings us to the tale of one captain's experience with a new flight attendant and an equally new copilot, both of whom had gotten themselves into a flight status with a tad too little education.

Part of the knowledge pilots and flight attendants are supposed to acquire when beginning a flying career with the airlines is this: Practicing emergency procedures with passengers aboard is a "no-no."

Certainly there are a number of exercises the pilots and flight attendants do—in fact, must do—to initially learn just what emergency procedures are; what parts of the aircraft are affected and how it relates to total safety. Appropriate airline employees are always expected to be current—"up to speed"—in their ability to handle any of their assigned emergency procedures. How the passengers are involved (and how to protect and care for them) is, of course, a major reason why the airline employees must be knowledgeable. But there can be no practicing unless the flight is a "non-revenue" trip.

In the "olden days," just because training programs were far from being what they are today, there were a few people who got into their new career without getting the word about everything expected of them.

Take this one DC-3 droning through the sky empty of passengers. (That's non-revenue, right?) The crew consisted of an experienced captain and his relatively inexperienced helpers, the copilot and flight attendant.

"Captain, I think I'd better have some help," revealed the copilot. "I'm just not sure of the complete procedure used in the DC3 when it's necessary to shut down one engine. And how about later when the pilot might like to restart it? Can we go over the whole bit while we've got an empty aircraft?"

"Sure," offers the captain, "I don't see why not, but I think it would be a good idea to tell the young lady back aft why we're going to kill one engine for a spell. It might surprise her if she looks outside and sees one of the engines is dead. Would you mind telling her what we're up to?"

"Gotcha," says the copilot, and saves himself and the relaxing lady a few steps by picking up the public address microphone. Then he proceeds to tell her the pilots' plan and quickly volunteers they are doing it because, as he said: "I'm still a bit new to all of this."

So the procedure of doing-what-when was laid on the new copilot, primarily meaning one engine's fuel supply was turned off and the big red button was pushed to stop the propeller's rotation.

With that accomplished—the propeller blades "feathered" edgewise into the onrushing windstream—both pilots talked about what had taken place and what would have to take place to restart the engine.

Our lady back in the cabin did look out, of course, for she had never seen a propeller stopped in mid-flight before. Now she knew what the procedure looked like and "precisely" why it had occurred. She must have said to herself: "I'll remember that."

Maybe a month later she got a chance to use that good information. The captain had just detected one of his engines had a major discrepancy and he shut the thing down, but had yet to make an announcement to the passengers. When a Navy pilot flying as a passenger sees one of the propellers come to a stop, he naturally is more than a little concerned. He points out the window and asks the young lady: "What's happened?"

"Oh," she looks out and casually replies, "the copilot is new at this.. they're just practicing."

As some of the readers know, it isn't always a problem with the airplane that makes a passenger nervous. Sometimes it's the weather. And it's a fair statement to say the DC-3 did not always produce the smooth-as-goosegrease ride. It couldn't if it had to fly right through the stormy or bumpy skies. But today's jets are no different when they are in that type of sky. Any aircraft will give you a smooth ride if it is above the turbulent weather. When the skies were rough the old DC-3 just couldn't fly high enough to escape into clear, comfortable air.

Even in Hawaii where flights are almost entirely over open water, if the sky is stormy, a trip can be just as choppy as a sea voyage on a wintery, windblown sea.

Captain Budd Murray, who started his island airline career in 1940, (and long since retired) made thousands of such trips. Perhaps once a month he would bear the wrath of a shook-up passenger who assumed a bumpy ride was primarily because Budd must have been a "terrible pilot."

Budd took all those complaints with grace. When a passenger voiced a gripe to Budd about "his poor flying," he or she was treated with the utmost courtesy. It was public relations at its very best.

Fred Eldridge recalls one such trip with Budd inbound to Honolulu from the island of Kauai. "It was a teeth-rattler," said Fred. "The Kauai channel was about as rough as it gets, and of course the old DC-3 couldn't fly high enough to get over the weather. If Budd wanted to get to Honolulu, he had to fly through it."

Fred remembers their arrival at Oahu's airport. All the passengers but one had disembarked. Fred was first to leave the cockpit and found this one remaining lady asking to speak to the captain. Fred told her he'd be out in just a moment. Which he was.

As soon as Captain Budd entered the passenger cabin, this lone lady lit into him with a venomous blast.. chewed on him up one side and down the other. Fred took it all in, and so did Budd.

Finally, she must have run out of breath. Budd gave the lady a gentle smile; measured his words carefully and calmly stated:

"Madam.. the good Lord makes the weather. If it's bumpy and bad.. all I can do is fly safely through it."

Early on in his career, ol' friend Charlie Barnard was flying copilot to a veteran called "Pop" Sterling. Pop's age and era was evident by the fact Orville Wright himself had issued Pop pilot license number 50. In United Airlines Pop was one of those legendary characters and no one had the temerity to give him much guff over how he flew the DC-3.

On a day when the entire flight path from Chicago to Denver was covered by rather low hanging clouds, Pop was doing all of his flying beneath them. By regulation, one thousand feet above the ground was the basic minimum altitude for all flights. Pop was bending the "regs" a little from time to time, and all the while each of the stations along their flight route kept reporting clouds down to 600 to 800 feet above the ground. The ceiling, as they call it, was low everywhere.

Pop was getting tired of trying to maintain 1,000 feet. Finally he turned to Charlie and said: "This is kind of silly. Put in a call to Denver and tell 'em we are proceeding at 500 feet."

Charlie knew that wasn't quite within the regulations. He also knew United's own rules about radio calls. If you made one, your name became a part of the message. And now, if he called in a message practically telling United "we're breaking the rules," it would have his name on it. Charlie protested, believing if it were wrong, adding his own name to Pop's illegal move wasn't the smartest thing he could do. But it did no good. Pop was adamant the message go out, so he simply told Charlie: "Put my name on the call."

And Charlie put in the call, still somewhat nervous about what the outcome might be. He said: "Sterling United 251, now proceeding to Denver at 500 feet."

Apparently the power of seniority kept Pop out of trouble, and, adds Charlie, "No one ever said anything to me about it."

If the DC-3 was a good airplane, it was also a fun aircraft—at least when it was a freighter or being ferried to and fro with no passengers aboard.

And there are some guys you enjoy having around, because they were fun, too. Captain Mike was one of those. Rarely anything but cheerful. Most of us never saw him when he wasn't ready for a dry, witty remark or didn't have time to pull a practical joke. Once in awhile, a friendly little gag for his day's partner aloft.

A good example is Mike and the DC-3 control cables. He had learned how to get at them from within the lavatory back in the tail section.

Mike was flying copilot for Captain Paul, the senior jokester. Paul, Mike and the stewardess were ferrying the plane empty back to the home base; a non-revenue flight, one that resulted in the crew being more relaxed. Paul was at the controls and Mike must have been a little bored. He told Paul he was going aft to the lavatory.

Shortly after Mike left the cockpit, Paul could feel the controls moving in a fashion he couldn't explain. Nothing violent, but Paul was experiencing some non-standard responses from the flight controls. Paul began to get more and more concerned, until finally he punched the stewardess call button. When she responded, Paul asked her to get Mike back to the cockpit.

She did that, and Mike comes back to his seat, dumb like a quiet fox who knows what's going on.

Paul tries to explain how it was to Mike, but admits he can't understand why all those strange little movements aren't happening anymore.

Of course Mike can't keep a straight face any longer; the smile keeps getting bigger and bigger until Paul gets the picture.

But Paul doesn't forget that incident; he saves the payback until they are on another ferry trip with no passengers aboard. Mike was at the controls, but decided a call of nature was more important than his turn as a pilot and asked Paul if he'd take over while he went aft to the lavatory. Nothing difficult about Paul; he was glad to.

Paul figured Mike wouldn't try to pull that same old trick again.. maybe on someone else, but not on Paul. He also figured if Mike really had a great urge for relief, he probably wouldn't take time out on the walk back aft to make small talk with the stewardess. Since Paul had taken that same trip a few hundred times in his career, he knew just how long it would take Mike to reach the lavatory and get himself unzipped.

About then Paul rather politely pushed, pulled, and yanked on the controls to the point that DC-3's tail section bounced quite unsteadily through the sky. It wasn't long before Mike came storming out of the lavatory and up the aisle, mad as.. well.. mad as a wet hen.

But Paul was such a pleasant person no one ever got really mad at him, least of all Mike. He got over it in quick fashion. If he was ever mad, he never stayed that way.

Of course, some things we never get over, and nothing could be much of a joke when the night freighter pilots had to slide by a casket or two in order to reach the cockpit. Like in the era of the Korean War when we lost a great many good men who, if they had had their druthers, wouldn't have chosen to ride home "in a box."

One airline in Hawaii had virtually all of the freight business then.. but the "casket" part of the company's operations was business the airline could have done without. If those deceased soldiers came from one of the neighbor islands, the airline had the none too pleasant responsibility of carrying them over that last body of water. Those trips took a lot of the joy out of flying that old DC3.

For the real night freighter crews, sundown meant their "day" was yet to begin. But in the years when this story took place—fortyfive years ago—night fliers in the islands were normally pretty relaxed. Air traffic was virtually nil and their obligations about how they conducted their business was more peaceful than daylight flying. Radio contacts still had to be made and navigation had to be just as accurate. The planes were on some sort of a prescribed clearance as to where they were going when, and usually how high.

But flying in those long, quiet hours of the night always gave the cockpit crew plenty of time to think.

Captain Bill and his copilot Jace were scheduled for a midnight departure out of Honolulu for Hawaii's largest island. Once their aircraft had been loaded, Bill and Jace, like all freighter pilots, sauntered out to inspect the condition of the aircraft. They also checked the placement and general condition of the cargo. If a casket was aboard, they couldn't help but give it a pat, remembering it was better to be delivering a casket rather than resting in one.

After they had completed their check of the aircraft and taken a good look at the loading of the cargo they would fly, they got the DC-3 fired up; received the air route traffic clearance and zoomed off into an otherwise quiet sky. Once they reached their cruising altitude they would have plenty of time to do much of nothing except pay attention to a few instruments and listen for a possible radio call.

It was one of Hawaii's few winter months, so the night air at the airport had been chilly. As the flight climbed out of the Honolulu area, our two quiet but thoughtful pilots couldn't help but dwell on the person in the casket; how did it all happen?.. what kind of a family did he have?.. what kind of a life he'd be missing in the future? In the dark of the night, the pilots' relaxed attitude made it easy to do some deep contemplation. Remembering the poor lad in the casket—a subject hard to ignore.

Naturally, up at a flight altitude of 7000 feet the temperature inside the DC-3's uninsulated cargo section definitely became uncomfortably cool. The pilots were warm enough. They both had jackets.. the cockpit instruments and a few dim lights added to their warmth. It was almost cozy. It was a black night but clear and quiet; nobody else in the sky; nothing very exciting to do but think.

As Bill told it, even the two engines outside lulled him into a "kinda dozy" feeling.

What lights the pilots had on up in the cockpit must've played some part in the thoughtful mood they were in. Very dim; nothing more than what came from the instrument panels. Mostly red and, under the right conditions—like this one, a little eerie.

Suddenly Jace sensed the presence of someone behind him. The feeling struck him as strange: There were three men aboard that DC-3 and one of them was in no shape to move around.

Very cautiously Jace peeks over his left shoulder and in the shadows sees this big guy, arms held high against the sides of the cockpit door.

Jace couldn't even find words.. probably unable to use them if he had. Best Jace could do, was carefully reach over and touch Bill on the arm, which roused Bill like a kick in the tail just because of his own thoughts about the guy in the casket.

The way Bill remembers it, Jace cocked his head a quarter turn toward his left shoulder, his mouth was open and moving but saying nothing, and Jace's eyes were rolled up and to his left in the general direction of the open cockpit door.

Bill said: "Even in the red light, Jace's face was only a pale pink and I finally got the message that I should look aft. Then I saw the guy. Scared me as much as it must have scared Jace."

Somehow one of the airline's cargo loaders was put aboard to help the destination crew with the freight handling, but that information never reached all the way to the cockpit; the pilots didn't know they had a live one back there.

The unknown crewman must have smiled or complained about how cold it was in the cabin. That broke the ice, Bill and Jace now reasonably sure they weren't having a pow-wow with the walking dead.

Both pilots knew when the old DC-3 had been up at 7,000 feet for twenty minutes or more, the cold night air at that altitude always soaked right through the skin of the aircraft. The cabin took on the temperature of an ice box, so it wasn't surprising the unscheduled loadmaster decided life up toward the cockpit ought to be a darn site warmer.

And it may have been warmer for him, but his surprise appearance sure put a chill on the cockpit crew!

Elderly.. but still a gentleman's aircraft

This Douglas DC-3 may be sitting in a pasture here, but the odds are this trusty aircraft is "ready to go." No other airliner has matched its amazing durability, capability and dependability. It filled a niche. The standard of many airlines for twenty years, the DC-3 has the distinction of flying commercially *longer* than any captain currently piloting a scheduled U. S. airliner has been *alive*.

TO REALLY GET THERE...

Navigation.. *good* navigation, is the key.

For those of you who weren't followers of the air travel scene during its early days, airlines didn't always breeze from point to point in bad weather or at night. Yet pilots were occasionally and unexpectedly forced to cope with those elements.

But initially there were no radio facilities to use for navigation, and few aircraft flight instruments that would aid the pilot in keeping the plane flying in a straight and level attitude. Basically what flight instruments planes had was narrowed down to one—a compass. Because the equipment needed had yet to be made available, the most experienced of the veteran pilots often flew in *verrry* questionable conditions and used their own private procedures for reaching one point from another.

Technically every flight went out under what we still call a VFR— visual flight rules—clearance. If they filed a clearance at all.

A very loose definition of VFR meant keep out of the clouds; be able to see a mile or so ahead; above all, don't get caught in or above the clouds without some way of getting back down through a clear spot.

The art of predicting the weather had yet to become a real science. (And many people think we still haven't learned to do it.) Some pilots thought V-F-R could stand for Very Foggy Ride or Visibility Falling Rapidly, but to the pilot who knew the route and countryside well, rain and clouds just added to the excitement of flying. At some time or other each pilot flew as he or she saw fit. Some stayed on the ground a lot; others said: "I'll chance it."

Before most of the rules about flying had yet to be developed, pilots took advantage of the nation's rail lines whenever they could. Those tracks were soon referred to as "the iron airway." Railroads had become so useful, pilots didn't hesitate to follow them anywhere. But, flying "by the tracks" sooner or later led to tunnels. As one old-timer said: "Pilots trying to fly through tunnels will find it's rather hard to see the tracks.. and, of course, your wings suddenly get shorter."

Pilots out in Hawaii never found any long distance railroad tracks connecting the islands, so they always had guidelines of their own. Those fellows flying the old Sikorsky amphibians in rainy weather would navigate between the islands using three simple elements: The clock, a compass and the sea.

Losing sight of land was not uncommon but no big deal. The experienced pilot who knew the time he left a certain point of land and also knew the exact compass heading, would also know the time it took to reach the next island even if he couldn't quite see the shoreline. He had learned that on the good days.

But during bad weather, there was more to it than watching the clock and the compass. The old-time pilot determined the wind's speed and direction from watching the sea, for the wind up to a 1,000 feet above the ocean is virtually the same wind a pilot could read from watching the waves or wavelets down on the surface.

And the color of the sea was most important. A gray-green or grayish-blue hue meant open ocean. If a pilot's timing across the channel was accurate, an island might be shrouded in rain but when muddy water began passing under the aircraft's nose, (run-off from sugar cane fields) it was a positive indication land was no more than one or two miles away. From that the pilot would waste little time in making an appropriate turn and follow the shoreline that would shortly appear through the rainy skies.

Reportedly one early-day pilot in Hawaii also used the length of his cigar ash over a given leg of his route to determine when some further action was necessary. With all due respects to a tall story, Hawaii's predictable weather and wind patterns made that method of navigation entirely possible—as long as that pilot always smoked the same brand of cigar.

Bush pilots in Alaska are something else! They have always made their own way. The average pilot in the lower 48 states would seldom leave the hangar in the kind of weather Alaskans view as being VFR.

If anyone learns how they navigate without roads, railroads and sometimes even without radios, please write the author and let him know.

How the early airmail pilots in the United States managed to survive the ordeals of delivering the U. S. Mail beginning as early as 1918 is also an interesting story.

Before acceptable passenger planes were introduced, the rugged, war-surplus open cockpit biplanes of the era began daily flights as mail planes.

With no radios, fliers had none of the well defined aerial maps pilots have been using for the past 60 years. And for nearly 15 years airmen lacked safe, dependable aircraft. In essence, their daring; their relatively meager skills as pilots, and the unseen caring of their Creator were the only real instruments of their success.

By the mid-twenties, the young adventurous pilots flew the mail even in darkness, retaining their self-imposed obligation: the contract to deliver mail between cities.

But soon over many routes they were being aided by lights that marked several of their usual aerial trails. Eager to continue fostering the air mail service, the government began developing a few major lighted airways.

Beacons were mounted every 10 to 12 miles between some of the nation's major cities; eventually across the full breadth of the United States. Searching white lights revolved in slow, flat circles over the landscape. Mounted on the same tower behind the white light, but pointed in the opposite direction, was another light, blinking in green, yellow or red, and identifying each specific beacon by one letter in Morse code. A green ID light meant a night-lighted airfield was close by. Yellow, told the pilot a non-lighted field was nearby. Over mountainous routes, most of the ID lights were red, indicating no suitable field was available. For the aviator flying at altitude on exceptionally clear nights, a string of four or five rotating beacons was a common and reassuring sight.

By the mid-1930's, navigation aids, called "low frequency radio range stations," were new innovations. Their importance lay in the direct support the stations offered to pilots trained to fly their planes by using flight instruments only—no visual contact with the earth.

The low-freq range station always transmitted two different radio signals (letters A and N in Morse code.) Those signals, each aimed in an entirely different direction, were sent out over the landscape. Where each of the A and the N signals transmitted had overlapped with equal audio intensity, (the "dit da" of one and the "da dit" of the other) melding of the two literally became the "beam." The result of those signals automatically produced four beams. Years ago when someone was said to be "right on the beam," you knew the speaker was a pilot or else hung around people who were.

If possible, the stations were placed near an airfield, even if it was no more than an emergency field. Sometimes because of mountainous country, the station's greatest value was something for the pilot to aim at when "the clouds were busy trying to hide all the rocks." The country's official airways all used these range stations, one or more of the radio beams oriented to lead right down the most suitable flight path.

For years the system's greatest disadvantage lay in the pilot's need to listen carefully to the radio signals repeated continuously. It was an ear-splitting hazard when heavy rain and electrical storms created severe static in the earphones. Often, pilots buried in the clouds for lengthy moments, would have been happier had they stayed at home.

By the mid-fifties, America had pretty well bracketed all of the air routes with a system lots of fliers still make good use of today. A high-frequency omni-directional radio station we call a VOR. A pilot can make (in a sense of the word) his or her own "beam." If the pilot desires to set a specific course to or from a VOR, he or she centers a movable needle on the plane's instrument panel. The aircraft is flying "on track" (i.e: over the chosen route) as long as the needle remains centered and its setting has not been changed. Listening hour after hour to static-filled low-frequency radios became unnecessary.

The time-honored means of sea or air navigation over long bodies of ocean was always the result of using well-known celestial entities... Venus, the moon, the sun, stars such as Polaris, Aldeberan and Betelguese. Then came a far-ranging electronic signal we termed LORAN.

But all of those systems are "old hat" in the modern aviation programs of today. Pin-pointing your plane's position by using information obtained from synchronized space satellites or by using a slightly less modern inertial guidance system can lead a pilot to an amazingly accurate landfall after his or her plane has flown thousands of non-stop miles.

Such is progress.

Despite that progress, people-type efforts still make it work—or allow it to fail.

Only a few decades ago when Pan American Airways was the most prestigious overseas airline, the author was a passenger inbound to Los Angeles from Honolulu. The aerial navigation had been near perfect; arrival time was as predicted, it had been a great flight.

Those waiting at the end of our journey were informed the airliner would dock at Gate 28. The anxious crowd watched curiously as the sleek jet taxied right past Gate 28 and docked at #29.

The friend meeting me, said later:

"Isn't that something? That captain could navigate that plane all the way across 2500 miles of ocean, but he couldn't find his way to the right gate!"

But even today, with all its high-tech methods, to err is human, and when that element enters the scene, anyone can suffer an embarrassing moment.. even those highly trained professionals in the aviation world. Fortunately those moments aren't too frequent, because the "business" looks at such careless mistakes with something other than kindness. (In air travel, safety is the first concern.)

Most pilots feel the greatest embarrassment in the flying game comes when a pilot lands without putting the landing gear in the down position. The next greatest might be landing at the wrongfield.

One of the latter (and most famous for its day) occurred in 1938 when this daring young fellow named Doug Corrigan took an old Curtiss Robin monoplane from New York, supposedly bound for California. He ended up landing in Ireland.

Widely publicized after that, hardly anyone called him anything but "Wrong Way Corrigan." And no one ever believed that landing was a mistake.

About the same year, friend Howard Phillips was landing in a locale that wasn't on his schedule. He wasn't terribly enthusiastic about it, but it certainly wasn't a mistake.

Howard, a long-time friend, has retired as an airline captain, but like everyone else there was a beginning to his career and this story is quite close to being the high-light.

When he was little more than a kid, this Massachusetts-born sailor had been stationed on a Pearl Harbor-based vessel for three or four years prior to the 1941 attack on Pearl Harbor. When his ship was tied up at the dock he was within earshot of airplanes, Hickam Army Air Base in one direction and Naval Air Station, Pearl Harbor, in the other. Almost as close was Honolulu's airport.

Howard's shipboard job wasn't all that exciting and the vessel to which he was assigned spent plenty of time in port. To the average sailor, it was a good ship for "liberty call," but no man aboard had ever "seen the world" from its deck.

Howard had started thinking about what life had to offer to a young man who really wanted to see something other than the inside of a Navy yard. He watched those airplanes come and go and then started giving thought about life in an airplane. To satisfy his interest, he took a short flight out of Honolulu Airport. It was convincing. He was hooked.

His trip to the airport set him straight on one thing: flying lessons weren't for free. And Navy pay in those days didn't get you much time in an airplane. Sixty bucks a month would buy 8 hours of instruction and leave you about five dollars for the other joys in life.

Howard thought the lessons were expensive but he liked flying enough to avoid thinking about price and he sent home for his savings. For the next few months he kept up the lessons and the solo practice periods. Once he had earned his Private Pilot's license it was only a small number of flight hours to earn what the federal government called the 'Limited Commercial' license. The required number of flight hours for that 'ticket' was fifty. During the first 50 hours, he alone paid for every hour he spent "boring holes through the air."

Having a Limited Commercial license entitled him to charge passengers for a local joy-ride within ten miles of his home field. He couldn't fly customers to any other airfield. It was simply an opportunity for an eager pilot to build up flight time. Flight time for the genuine-go-anywhere Commercial license, yet do it on someone else's money.

Howard had access to a 1930's model trainer—a Waco biplane that could carry a total of 3 people. He convinced any number of daring souls that an aerial environment was almost as safe as their living room.

Two adventurous females of Howard's acquaintance decided "he talked a good flight;" they really would like to fly over the city.

"It's a good deal," said Howard, "because with two of you going at once, I'll charge each of you just a dollar and half for thirty minutes. Why don't you gals do that?"

"We don't do that because we don't have $1.50," said the sweet young things, coyly, "but we'll have it next week."

"O.K.," said Howard, "tell you what I'll do. We'll go flying today and you can pay me next week."

That was fine with the girls. Howard and his passengers all piled into the Waco and took off.

Everything went okay until they had passed over the city of Honolulu. About that time the top of one cylinder cracked off and Howard's only engine threw a pushrod. With an engine like that, the biplane lost practically all interest in flight. It was still controllable, but had a disenchanting tendency to slowly head for the ground.

That demanding situation didn't give Howard any chance to explain the whole deal to his passengers. He was too engrossed in finding a suitable landing area, saving lives and a valuable airplane.

Howard was not too happy with his problem. While he may have simulated a dozen engine failures under the guidance of his instructor—practicing all the way down to a point just above an empty field somewhere—*this* was the real thing!

But, as luck would have it, the place Howard selected for his forced landing was an area he had driven through only a few days before.. a section of flat land on the Waikiki side of a newly opened street. It had looked so good from his car, he remembered thinking: "what a great place to land a plane if you ever had to."

Howard's engine was just barely producing 1100 RPM—only a portion of what it took to keep the plane in the air—and that bare field looked even better than sex to a jailhouse bum!

Howard took a good look at the wind direction; hardly any different from what it had been at the airport. As he passed over the edge of the city, turning toward that spot of cleared land, he became aware the plane had been sinking faster than he had expected. He cut short his approach, angling in toward the selected site; just hoping to reach what appeared to be that smooth, graded area.

When he did so, he caught sight of power lines crossing his flight path.

He had no choice! Hit the throttle and hope the ruptured engine still had enough get-up-and-go to avoid those wires! *"Whew!.. close."* After crossing the power lines, he had the field made and he let the Waco settle in.

Stopping the roll-out before he ran out of space was the next concern. Howard wasn't too keen on the quality of braking he could get out of that Waco. It had a strange set-up that found a brake lever attached to the throttle control. Pulling on the lever, then pushing one or both of the rudder pedals gave you all the available braking. Howard's earlier flights in the Waco told him that wasn't likely to be very much.

But Howard pulled on that lever and stomped on those two rudder pedals for all he was worth. He did so well the wheels skidded for 75 feet and he came to a stop within six feet of one of Hawaii's many coconut palms!

The girls and Howard had just finished climbing out of the plane when a Honolulu city policeman entered the scene.. He wanted to know what Howard and his plane were doing there, and, like a cop who stops you for vehicle traffic violations, he wanted to see Howard's license.

Howard believes that's the first—and most likely the last time—he could expect to have his pilot's license checked by a police officer.

Howard told him the story and the officer said he'd call in and have the owner of the plane notified.

About that time the officer looked around for the girls just to get a statement from them.

They had disappeared.

Howard had heard of gals having to walk home before, but none he knew ever did it from a ride in an airplane.

During World War II landing at the wrong airfield probably happened a hundred times. There were many young, inexperienced aviators, and new airfields sprang up like toadstools. A few such pilots even made the mistake of landing at enemy airfields.

One Navy pilot was flying to the west coast for the first time; his destination: the Alameda Naval Air Station. After a long, tiring flight across the United States, this pilot spotted a rather sizable airport at the water's edge. "Ah-ha," he says, "there it is." Switching to the standard Navy radio frequency, he told Alameda tower he was six miles east awaiting landing clearance. Alameda had other planes in their immediate vicinity, but apparently none in their landing pattern. Unconcernedly, tower gave this newcomer a clearance to land on the runway headed northwest.

"Roger," said the incoming pilot, and made his landing.

Shortly after landing, the new arrival asked Alameda tower for instructions on where he should taxi.

Alameda tower replied: "Where are you now? Over."

"This is Navy such-and-such here on the runway. Over."

"Sorry, we don't see you. What type aircraft? Over."

The newcomer told the controller who then answered: "I don't have you in sight. Are you sure you're at Alameda? Is it possible you might have landed just south of here at Oakland?"

Long silence on the other end terminated in an eventual response: "Sorry, Alameda."

(Oakland Municipal was down the bayfront; its primary runway oriented similarly to Alameda's duty runway.)

So it took another five minutes for that pilot to circle over the Alameda Naval Air Station, and ask its tower for landing clearance—again.

Another happened at night in Ohio some 20 years ago. A jet airline crew (with passengers) received landing clearance from Tower at their scheduled arrival airport. Up ahead an airport sighted; its lighting appearing adequate, and the landing went fine. Both pilots were quick to notice, however, their runway had ended all too soon, requiring maximum reverse thrust on the jet engines and heavy use of brakes.

But the plane stopped safely and the crew began communicating on the radio again, finally learning the horrible truth: they were at an airfield technically and legally unsuitable for large jets; their scheduled airport a half dozen miles away.

To pack more egg on his face, the captain learned his aircraft couldn't take off. The runway was too short. The passengers were eventually off loaded without the usual appropriate courtesies, finishing their flight by bus.

Highlighting this entire subject is the *AIRWAYS* magazine (Jan/Feb 1996) mention about an air carrier DC-10 inbound from the U. S. to Frankfurt, Germany.

After a long flight over the Atlantic the airliner had passed both the Ireland and the London air traffic control centers smartly, seemingly in accordance with their flight plan. Then things went awry. Earlier in the hour before they finally landed, erroneous transmissions between traffic control centers and the DC10 had altered the plane's routing. No one, neither air traffic controllers nor the airliner's cockpit crew had caught the error. Input to the computers (apparently all unintentional by air traffic controllers) resulted in some changes to the airliner's flight plan.

In the cabin, "241 passengers and the flight attendants watched" the electronic map, puzzled at the 'changes' in their re-routing. "Reportedly," states *AIRWAYS,* "some flight attendants speculated the plane had been hijacked, but none of them called the cockpit."

By FAA rules, which forbid non-emergency interruptions to the cockpit crew during a descent/approach, the flight attendants never considered the series of events to be an "emergency" and did not call the cockpit.

Somewhere over Belgium, "the crew called `Frankfurt Approach,'" but the....controllers [on the ground] never corrected the radio transmissions" as they should have. The flight crew was instructed to descend using a local air navigation station for which the crew requested a frequency.

Shortly thereafter, the flight crew had almost completed their final approach; had broken out of the low hanging clouds, and were lined up on a runway, ready for landing. Once visually spotting the airfield, the captain apparently realized that in spite of staring at a perfectly aligned runway, he *wasn't* looking at Frankfurt.

And, having already reached the maddening conclusion he was in the wrong, *AIRWAYS* reported, the captain evidently decided it was 'just one of those days' and terminated his flight right where he had landed—Brussels, Belgium—some 200 miles from Frankfurt.

Then there are those days when it seems "you jes' cain't get there from here."

Like in the example of Flight 1627 outbound from Detroit to Minneapolis shortly after noon. At the time of departure, Minneapolis was a destination without any serious weather problems. En route, that picture was to change.

Cruising comfortably over Lake Michigan, the aircraft was asked to deviate slightly to provide better spacing between aircraft. In a matter of minutes trip 1627 was routed back on its original course. The flight might get into Minneapolis two or three minutes later than scheduled, but no big deal. The flight was still headed for Eau Claire, Wisconsin, an intermediate navigation fix for aircraft due to land at Minneapolis (the place where there was "only a chance thunderstorms might be found in the area.")

In the interim, Mother Nature decided things weren't lively enough in Minnesota, and big bumpy clouds that send sparks down upon the populace had suddenly shown up in force. The area over Minneapolis was being bisected by a long line of thunderstorms; that same line went up toward the north and down south into Iowa. While lightning battered the earth—and threatened things above the earth—the clouds that ignite that lightning weren't moving off their targets. If movement was apparent, it was extremely slow.

And thunderstorms are "chancy" creatures. There's a chance even just one can louse up your whole day. When there is a way to avoid them, the wise pilot does exactly that.

From the pilots' compartment of Flight 1627, the passengers heard: "...and the possibility exists, ladies and gentlemen, we *may* be delayed." No sooner had that announcement been completed when the aircraft received three more weather reports. Two were discouraging accounts about growth of additional thunderstorms throughout the midwestern section of the nation. The third made it clear the then current storm over Flight 1627's destination was intensifying.

Those reports were immediately amplified by a message from Minneapolis-St.Paul: "All aircraft to MSP please note the airport is closed due to weather..." Followed by instructions to those aircraft assigned to a holding pattern over Eau Claire to remain there; "Flight 1627 to hold at flight level 3-5-0." (For the uninitiated, 3-5-0 is short for 35,000.)

While in the holding pattern over Eau Claire, with what seemed to be a fleet of aircraft, radio calls to and from the air traffic control center were heard constantly. Eventually, several of the aircraft holding there left for airfields elsewhere because of diminishing fuel supplies, and trip 1627 was directed to a new holding point only 55 miles northwest of Minneapolis. In essence the message was: "When the storm center drifts further east, we'll bring you in from the west." (If the storms over MSP move, it will be toward the east.)

But the storm over MSP does not move by the time trip 1627 arrives at its new holding position and the airport at Minneapolis is still not open for traffic.

"Not good," says 1627's captain, "our fuel supply is almost at the point where we, too, will have to divert to some other airport," and he begins a radioed discussion with his dispatcher in Minneapolis.

During the course of the decision making, the first officer has been making an announcement to the passengers: "...due to the weather...it is possible we will have to divert...I will give you an update within a few minutes. Thank you."

Captain and dispatcher make a decision: Go to Grand Forks, North Dakota; land, refuel and hope for a later break in the Minneapolis weather. Flight 1627 subsequently receives that clearance. Out goes another report to the passengers about a further delay only the more serious safety-minded folk appreciate.

"Well.. there goes the ol' ballgame," thought the first officer, who had plans for the evening. "We'll never get to Minneapolis in time to make it."

One hour after the plane was due in MSP, trip 1627 is landing in North Dakota, more than 200 miles away. The aircraft is not alone. Two other planes have also arrived and need fuel. But additional delays occur because each of the trucks required refilling before fully supplying all the waiting aircraft.

Wisely, the captain asks the passengers to remain aboard, for if the total passengers from three aircraft deplane, it means 500 will be coexisting in an air terminal capable of holding only 100.

Meantime, weather conditions over Minneapolis are improving though additional thunderstorms have developed over the route between there and Grand Forks.

Frustration and concern exists among some of the passengers. Two—a mother and her sick child—were headed for a St. Paul hospital; the child scheduled for a critical bone marrow transplant in the morning. From Grand Forks the airline arranges for direct communication with the hospital, and adjustments for the child's procedure are made.

After another forty-five minutes wait for a second fuel truck, Flight 1627 taxies out shortly after six p.m. The first officer announces: "...the weather en route to MSP is likely to be occasionally turbulent...flight time to MSP is expected to be fiftyfive minutes...we thank you for your patience."

Already beginning to dodge thunderstorms over the assigned route to the navigational fix at Brainerd, trip 1627 is fifteen minutes outbound from Grand Forks when the air traffic control center calls. Their message: "1627.. Advise when you are ready to copy holding instructions."

"Holding??...C'mon!" The captain and first officer both sigh the same response. Neither pilot can believe what they heard.

The first officer thinks: "Hey.. we've been there and done that. But who cares about baseball anyhow?"

The first holding circuit of the dinner hour places 1627 in the near center of a dying thunderhead. Dying, but definitely not dead, was the finding of the captain and he requests a different area. A new location near Brainerd was chosen by the air traffic people. Its only fault was the time required for 1627 to remain "boring holes in the sky and going nowhere." That obligation lasted twenty-five minutes when a new instruction squawked over the aircraft radio: "Flight 1627 cleared to Minneapolis..." and the message adds their specific route and frequency to use.

The first officer had no sooner switched frequencies, when the new controller told 1627: *(You guessed it!)* "Advise when ready to copy *holding instructions.*" In their best French, both pilots voiced their comments to each other.. it would have been 'politically incorrect' to say it over the air.

But their luck was changing, and 1627 had made only two circuits of the holding pattern before they were descending as if on a spiral staircase into an approach to Minneapolis runway #11-left.

From departure in Detroit, Flight 1627 had been en route—or working hard at it—for nearly six hours. The flight crew had fully expected a hardened, growling group of passengers to deplane in MSP.

Not so. Thankful to be safe on the ground—and at their final destination—every passenger voiced satisfaction for the flight crew's effort and were particularly appreciative of having been kept fully informed as the flight progressed.

Well... maybe there *is* a better word than 'progressed.

Back in July 1979 many citizens in the tiny northern Wyoming town of Buffalo were looking for an excuse for a civic event... a celebration; a town-wide party, but not like "Pioneer Days." Every other little town had been doing them for years; it was old stuff.

Some said, "Too much the same. We oughta come up with something original."

Someone "up there" must have been in the mood to help, for lo and behold... "Surprise!" A Boeing 737 jet landed at the municipal airport, totally unannounced and laden with passengers.

"Strange," agreed Buffalo locals, "we don't usually have jet airliners landing here. In fact, this is the first one."

Everybody in town went out to take a look at this one-of-a-kind event. Most people took it as the most excitement they'd had in Buffalo since grandpa was a boy. With a tongue-in-cheek flavor, the local newspaper heralded the jet's arrival: BUFFALO GETS ITS FIRST JET SERVICE! — and probably its last.

It really put Buffalo on the map, for the jet's correct destination had been Sheridan, Wyoming, 25 miles to the north.

The town welcomed the sudden influx of visitors, but the citizens really got wound up on the instantly famous captain who caused the whole affair. He had brightened everyone's life but his own! The town folk decreed a day in late July would thereafter be celebrated as his day; "Lowell Furgeson Day." And they let the embarrassed captain know he would always be invited.

For some reason the captain's airline didn't get too enthusiastic over Buffalo's excuse for a celebration.

"Well, one thing for sure," said an air-minded local, "the captain is a darn good pilot to have landed that big plane on such a small runway!"

Of course, the captain probably took that as rather "faint praise," because he knew his airline and the FAA watchdogs wouldn't be looking at the situation in the same light. He guessed if they let him fly at all, he'd be demoted to copilot.

Furgeson's jet was not legal to take off from the Buffalo municipal airport — at least not with passengers or in accordance with routine regulations, so passengers were bussed and a special crew came to fly the 737 to a more suitable airfield.

Later, after Furgeson got what he expected — retraining and a year's duty as copilot — he once again began flying as captain. He showed up in Buffalo at least once for "his" day — without his 737. One last comment: The airline never again scheduled him for any trips to Sheridan, Wyoming.

THE MILITARY: *NOT* A PIECE OF CAKE

Most folks in this day and age don't realize we used to fly fixedwing aircraft off Navy battleships and cruisers. Battleships are long gone as active vessels, and both ships began depending upon radar to do the scouting missions accomplished by what World War II personnel called "float" planes.

Float planes were so named because.. well.. they had to float when landing on water. It was the only choice they had. (Actually, they were probably called that because they used one big fat float instead of landing gear.) The Navy's leading float plane when WWII began was the single engine, two-seated OS2U, or "Kingfisher." The aircraft was usually launched from a catapult—literally fired off the ship—and, after landing in the sea, retrieved by a crane.

During the air battles in the vastness of the Pacific Ocean, the OS2U proved *verrry* precious to a sizeable number of carrier pilots who had ditched in the sea, unable to return to their ship. When the Kingfisher pilots were aloft—but not in—air battles with the Japanese forces, it was the slow-moving, underpowered Kingfisher which often came to the rescue of downed pilots.

In one such rescue, the float plane landed among several lifejacketed flight crew members. Some, unable to find space in the rear cockpit, were happy to ride up on top of the wing, or on the float, itself. The Kingfisher pilot couldn't fly with a crowd of soaking wet pilots and rear-seat gunners hanging on wherever they could, so he just stayed on the water and began taxiing back toward his own ship. The ship was not in sight before a U.S. submarine observed the OS2U struggling against the forces of the sea. The sub surfaced and came along side. While the carrier crewmen were grateful the float plane had shown up, they were happy as hell to jump aboard the sub. After some deliberation, the pilot of the float plane and the skipper of the sub decided the Kingfisher's low fuel supply would keep it from flying very far. The trusty float plane was consigned to Davy Jones' locker—courtesy of the sub's heavy deck gun.

During the early half of the war, the Navy decided the Kingfisher wasn't good enough for our boys. A new plane was ordered. It came equipped with an engine with far greater power, but was a float plane with only one seat: the pilot's.

The newer aircraft was the Curtiss-built SC-1, the "Seahawk."

Pilots who were to fly the new float plane—and who fully understood a scout/observation plane's mission—had difficulty understanding the truth about *why* the single-seater Seahawk came to be.

It couldn't perform some of the missions the Kingfisher had been doing. In comparison to its predecessor, it was faster and looked sportier, but it was also heavier; had less range, and was less durable.

Was it possible Curtiss, the famed old supplier of numerous Navy airplanes (including the very first) just needed the business? They had built the WWII dive bomber, the "Helldiver," and while it was faster than those dive bombers available at the outset of war, it was heavier and considerably more difficult to maintain.

"Strange," thought some of the few pilots who flew the SC-1, "that's just about the difference between the Seahawk and the older Kingfisher. And to top it off, it can't fly as far."

Floatplane pilots felt strongly about their ability to pop down on the ocean's surface and pluck a fellow pilot out of King Neptune's realm. With the advent of the new SC-1, they had lost that capability—until someone in authority tried to rectify the situation. That "someone" decided to install a stretcher-like device in the empty fuselage behind the pilot. "At least it was installed in our planes," said Jim Lotzgesell, of the cruiser USS Nashville.

"But," added Jim, "the pilot's seat was blocking access, so, they reconfigured the seatback. After being unlocked from the upright position, it could bend forward. The theory was: the pilot could land, pick up the survivor, tilt the seat forward and let him climb in behind the pilot's seat and lie on the stretcher. Then away we'd go. Well.. that *was* the theory. I don't know if anyone was ever rescued with an SC-1. However, I do know that at least once, with a man in the fuselage compartment,an open sea takeoff was tried out—with spectacular results." Spectacular alright, but not good.

Whenever it was near payday, it had been a custom on the Nashville for the air division to fly the paymaster into port in order for him to have enough funds to pay the crew immediately upon arrival.

"The head man in the money department "volunteered" his assistant to try out the new "passenger procedure" in the SC-1," and, said Jim, "I volunteered to do the flying. We had about a day to go before reaching Pearl Harbor. In the interim, the senior aviator and myself decided not to make a catapult shot with a man in the back of that airplane. We thought it would be less dangerous if I made a rough water (open sea) take off instead."

In the event of a crash, (remembering the most likely locale for such a happening would be the sea) the worst imaginable hazard was having the "stretcher" passenger trapped behind the pilot's seat. There was no other exit. The pilot had to quickly remove himself from the seat and unlock it, enabling the seatback to bend forward before he himself left the aircraft.

"As it turned out," Jim said, "our theories on the subject were exactly right."

The paymaster was about to become the Nashville's first guinea pig—riding on the stretcher. After he climbed in, pilot Jim entered and returned his seatback upright, locked the latch and secured himself in the cockpit, ready for takeoff.

The ocean swells were from four to six feet high. High enough to question the Seahawk's ability to reach flying speed prior to having the aircraft beaten to pieces from impact with the waves.

"We bounced several times; each time the plane wanted to porpoise into a nose down position, and gradually (due to the extreme torque of the engine) the aircraft moved off the projected course of takeoff. I finally got the nose pointed up and we came off the water. We were 30 to 50 feet in the air and I thought she was going to make it, then the plane started to roll to the left and went into a nose down attitude. I pulled back on the stick to pull the nose up and tried to roll to the right. The pressure on the stick was over powering and she kept going over to the left. I took my feet off the rudder pedals and braced them on the instrument panel, pulling back on the stick and to the right. The nose came up but we were falling off to the left in a flat skid. I knew that was "it".. we were going in, so I chopped the power and kept pulling back on the stick to keep the nose up. (I think getting the nose up saved our lives.)

Finally, the worst happened. The plane slapped harshly sideways into a wave, snapping off the left elevator and stabilizer. Simultaneously, the main float cracked off and the left wing snapped, as well. We were done for!"

Jim immediately chopped the throttle; popped his seat and shoulder straps; rose out of the seat and, unlocking the back of his seat, yelled to the paymaster: "Get the hell outta here!"

The paymaster was ready and moved faster than anyone has ever seen him move on payday. He didn't have to go far, the aircraft almost entirely underwater, the cockpit completely submerged. Up and out was an urgent plan in Jim's mind, as well. Unfortunately, he and the Seahawk were already below the surface when more trouble ensued.

Jim recalled: "I was still facing aft, and when I left the cockpit my parachute pack got hung up on the windshield. I went back down and shook it loose and started to swim away from the aircraft which was sinking rapidly. But now an antenna wire, still attached to the tail, kept hooking on to me; dragging me down with the plane! By the time I finally broke free I was so far under water I couldn't see light. I didn't know which way was up, I only knew I wanted to go the opposite direction the Seahawk was going."

The swim up to the surface, laden with the parachute pack and all the accessories was a long one. After Jim broke the surface, he swore he couldn't have held his breath another second.

"Things had happened so fast," Jim recalled, "I hadn't even had time to take a big breath before going under."

Once on the surface, Jim looked for the paymaster. "He was floating in his life jacket about ten or fifteen feet away from me. Then I found my jacket wouldn't hold air. Apparently snagging it on the antenna wire had cut holes in it. Struggling to stay afloat, I realized I still had my parachute pack with me and there was a life raft in it. I pulled it out and unfolded it, but when I tried to inflate it my hands were too wet to get a good grip on the handle. It was a nice slippery plastic one you had to turn like a faucet."

"I almost laughed over the irony.. someone designed a life raft that required dry hands to get the damned thing to work. I wondered if *anything* was going to work that day!"

Jim figured out how he could still put air in the life raft with the hand pump that came with it, even though it, too, had been so carefully packed and protected, it became a nightmare to get it operational. Fortunately, Jim had received special training on how to survive from a sinking aircraft. (Jim was thankful he "didn't fall asleep in *that* class!") "Surprising," he said, "to discover just how difficult it is to get into a life raft in the open sea. It is not a task for the uninitiated."

The Nashville, less than two miles away, was already lowering a motor whale boat. Within fifteen minutes the water-soaked aeronauts had been picked up. Both suffered nothing more than a few bruises.

Jim stated the ship's Executive Officer came down to the dispensary to see how each of us were doing. "He thanked me for getting the paymaster out first. After he saw us crash, he thought: 'How am I going to explain this to [the paymaster's] wife?'"

Jim always wondered why—with all of the senior officers aboard that ship—someone didn't come forward and ask "these two junior pilots" if we weren't completely out of our minds!

Well.. we all have at least one story about a day we could have done without.

In years back, Bob was a flight instructor but still a relatively inexperienced Navy ensign. In a short time, many of this officer's contemporaries saw him as a cool, confident individual. But one sultry Florida night Bob received the first real test of his ability to handle responsibility, an undertaking the military loves to assign.

Frankly, it put him "on the hook" for *anything* that might go wrong. He was to be the tower duty officer monitoring a group of night flying students. It meant he was in charge of what went on in the airfield's traffic pattern and on the airfield operational area. He was in the control tower in the event the controller needed some command decisions. Bob was to take action if anything out of the ordinary occurred.

"Every decision I make," thought Bob, nervously, "is likely to be mine alone. I'm it. Only the Command Duty Officer (CDO) really has any greater responsibility. And he's not where the action might be. He's sittin' by a phone." Bob wondered about himself—and imagined what he might be in for.

And events far beyond the ordinary happened on that night.

Numerous planes, flying in small, tight groups called 'night formation,' eventually returned to the airfield landing pattern; each pilot intent on getting his plane safely on the ground.

Suddenly a red signal flare arced into the night. "Uh-oh" was Bob's first thought, realizing why the flare had been fired and by whom. The "wheel-watch" man at the approach end of the runway had done his thing with the flare because one of the incoming planes— supposedly ready to land—had failed to lower the landing gear. The plane was one of the several thousand 1940's era trainers the Navy called an SNJ.

Bob hoped against hope the errant pilot of the plane had caught sight of the bright red flare, but before he could even finish his thought, a splash of sparks silhouetted the single engine plane as it ground to a stop on the runway below.

"Sir! Aircraft bellied in!" shouted the tower control man. "I see it," replied Bob, somewhat frantic in his attempt to push the buttons that would guarantee reaction by the crash and rescue crew. Trucks with sirens and flashing red lights responded almost immediately.

Bob gratefully observed there was no fire around the aircraft and the pilot had removed himself from the plane. In Bob's eyes both were good signs. He was especially grateful the crash crew had been on the ball when the call came for their services. No one could raise hell with him about their rapid reaction.

But then he recalled something in the instructions about calling the duty officer for the squadron involved. According to procedure, that junior officer had to know; the air station's CDO had to know, and was there anyone else??

About then the tower controller gave Bob more news:

"Sir, There's a fire on the field!"

"Fire?.. How'd we get a fire?" barks Bob, as he wheeled to view the latest problem.

"It's a grass fire," said the towerman, "See?.. over by the fence."

"Okay, yes, I see it.. Call the fire department!" And Bob immediately surmised the "why" and the "what;" a grass fire probably started by the unspent red flare when it fell to earth.

Bob now had something new to add to his phone call to the CDO. In preparation for any quiz he might receive from the CDO, Bob made a quick check with the tower controlman: "You got the fire department okay?.. they're on their way?"

"Yessir, I see 'em going out now, sir."

Bob resumed his efforts to place a call to the CDO. When that senior officer was reached, Bob carefully relayed all of the current information: "A wheels-up landing, sir, on runway 3, sir. The pilot appears——"

"What squadron was it?" snaps the CDO

Bob tells him, also that the pilot appears okay; no fire on the aircraft, but we've got one out near..."

"What?? "

"——the southwest corner of the field, sir."

"Why didn't you tell me?"

"Uh, it just now started, sir. It seems to be a grass fire, sir."

"And?? exclaims the CDO.

"And the fire crew is on their way out there.. in fact, I think they are at the scene now, sir"

"You *think* so? Don't you *know?*"

"Uh, yessir.. I'm sure. I can see the truck."

"How about the crane?" asks the CDO. "Did you tell them to get that damned aircraft off the runway?"

"Uh..yessir, we're doing that, sir."

"And what are you going to do about those other aircraft? Let 'em run out of gas before they get a chance to land?"

"Nnno, sir. Can't we land them on the other runway, sir?"

"Only if you know the wind conditions are suitable. Are you sure you won't have to divert them to another air station?"

Bob wasn't sure. He hadn't yet thought of that, but he would now. "We're preparing for that possibility, sir," he replied with a steadier voice.

"Well.. keep me informed" said the CDO in a none too friendly manner.

Bob began his efforts to find out how the crane was coming along in its removal of the disabled SNJ. The craneman, already informed by the crash & rescue crew, had responded quickly and within minutes the self-powered machine edged its way into view and onto the runway to retrieve the crunched aircraft.

"Sir, crash and rescue reports the pilot is fine and they estimate twenty five minutes until the runway is clear," volunteered the tower controlman.

"Good news," exclaimed Bob, "those other aircraft will be needing to land within the next thirty to forty five minutes or so. Hand me the tower log, would you?" Quickly, Bob scrawls notes in the logbook, reminding himself to call any nearby air station to learn if their runways are open in the event he is forced to divert the planes that remain aloft. He looks toward the airfield and sees the crane is on the scene. A crew is trying to hook a sling to the SNJ. "At least they look as though they are doing okay," he mutters.

"Maybe it's time to call the CDO again.. tell him the crane is definitely at the scene," thinks Bob.

He dials and after two rings came a reply: "C-D-O here."

"Sir, this is the Tower duty officer again, I've finally got a breather. Regarding the SNJ.. the crane should have the runway clear in another fifteen to twenty min——"

"Sir," interrupted the controller. "Sir.. Just a minute sir, the crane broke down, sir."

Bob turned his head from the phone, looked in despair at the tower controller, then back to his report to the CDO.

"Sir.. we've just gotten a report from the deck. There's a problem with the crane."

"Well, find out what the problem *is,* Ensign, and get it *fixed!*" retorts the CDO.

"Yessir, I don't know what's wrong, but we'll find out and call you back, sir" responded the harassed ensign. "Oh sir?.. the fire on the field is out."

"That's nice, isn't it?" replies the CDO, with what Bob felt was with a touch of sarcasm.

Within moments the crash crew reported to Tower the craneman knew what his trouble was and "thinks it will be set to go in 30 minutes."

"Thirty minutes!" thought Bob aloud. "The planes up there will *really* be getting short on gas! Holy smoke.. what are we gonna do with the planes still in the air?" Then to the tower controlman: "Did you find out about a field that can take some of these planes we have?"

"No sir, I thought you were going to do it, sir."

Bob sighed "Yeah.. I was, wasn't I? But we know mainside is open, don't we?"

"Yessir. Chevalier's open."

Meantime, the returning planes kept circling the field, every minute getting closer to fuel starvation. The fact there were many planes being flown by students weighed heavily on Bob's mind.

"For God's sake, the ball is really in my court," he thought.

None of the students had much night flying experience; few were familiar with the availability of other airfields in the surrounding area. Then one of the circling planes suddenly reported his fuel was getting low and that he would like to divert to another airfield. Bob cleared him to go to Chevalier, but the response was less than encouraging.

"How do I find it?" replied the pilot.

Bob told the controller to tell the pilot: "Fly south. When you reach the ocean, turn right and fly the coastline until you see the main air station on your right. We'll tell them you're coming."

Then Bob thought about his airfield's other runway, and checking the current wind, he read the anemometer. The wind was much stronger than usual. It was 18 knots and blowing right down the runway that was blocked. Using the remaining runway would mean having all planes land in a strong crosswind. "Holy bejesus," he said, "we've gotta get that plane off the runway or send the others to mainside!"

Next, a student pilot flying solo, suddenly discovered how dangerously low his fuel had become, and came close to panic. He radioed "Mayday, Mayday!" the emergency call for help and requested immediate guidance. He knew he had to land soon but where?, how?

"Holy mackerel!" uttered the haggard ensign, "I've got no time to call the CDO for advice. They'll probably hang my butt for this!"

The tension had built to a new high, but Bob quickly made a decision. He had the tower controlman advise the nervous pilot about the strong crosswind, but cleared him to land on the airfield's other runway— conditions highly unfavorable for a student flyer. Bob literally chewed nails watching him land; afraid the student might ground-loop. "Hold 'er, kid," said Bob under his breath. "Keep it straight.. Keep it straight.. You *got* it!" The landing went well. Bob sank into a chair.. the first comforting moment of the night.

Bob called the CDO for the third time, reporting his latest on the crane repair. "Yessir, I'll look forward to seeing you when you arrive, sir." Bob cradled the phone and told the controller: "The Command Duty officer will be here soon."

Within twenty minutes the repaired crane had cleared the wrecked SNJ; the remaining night fliers had landed on the duty runway, and Bob saw the CDO pounding up the last flight of stairs and entering the tower's cab.

Bob and both of the tower personnel stood and saluted the station's senior duty officer whose only immediate reaction was a salute in return and the query:

"Ensign.. give me an update. Is everything in the log?"

Bob, unsure of how things looked to the CDO, apparently provided the officer with satisfactory responses, then heard the CDO say "Okay, son. I'll take it from here."

Relieved of his duty, he was reasonably sure of only one thing: It was one of those days he should have stayed in bed!

A great many of us have days and nights like that, but could any be more severe than this tale about a Navy friend named Don?

Being a flier in the armed services frequently demands more from an individual than just being brainy, skillful and healthy. Don had all those qualities. Yet if you had seen Don make his "special" type of landing at Columbus, Ohio, in 1967, you would never expect to see him on the golf course ever again—never expect to see him *ever!* Don had just ejected from a Navy jet.. blasted out—at ground level— with horrendous results!

On that day he would have been better off if he, too, had stayed in bed. As you might have guessed, for months after the incident in which Don and his big twin-engine, supersonic carrier plane went their separate ways, he spent *days* in bed—a hospital bed.

Read this tale, if you please. It's almost too unbelievable.. it'll make you believe any of the flights you ever take will likely be a "piece of cake."

Don was the Navy's representative at the factory in Columbus where these high-tech "super" birds were being made. There he flew a plane with the military designation of RA-5C, then one of the most modern aircraft in the Navy's inventory. Part of his duty at the Columbus factory was delivering planes to Florida, something Don had done several times.

"The usual routine," said Don, "was fly the new machine into the Sanford Naval Air Station, then catch an airline flight back to Ohio. This time however, one of the RA-5C's on the field was still under warranty and it had developed a problem. The people at Sanford asked me and my rear-seat man if we would take it back to the factory."

Don, who wasn't keen on flying all the way to Ohio in a one- or two stop airliner, said he welcomed the idea. "But," he added, "I wanted to know *why* the aircraft had to go back."

"Lousy paint job," said the officer at Sanford.

"How's that?" asked Don.

"Every time the plane went supersonic, the paint started stripping off," was the reply.

Don didn't have any objection to accepting the plane if it freed him from airline passage, but he had to inspect the aircraft for anything more serious than a bad paint job. And he did find there had once been a problem with one engine's "fire warning lights." Only recently those lights suddenly started shining brightly in a pilot's eyes. In the RA-5C the unusual and continuous display of such lights was considered so worrisome, the flight operations manual dictated the best course of action was to abandon the aircraft. Obviously when it had happened previously, the pilot had decided against giving up on the airplane; rode it home to Sanford, and the mechanics found what appeared to be the difficulty.

"Okay," said Don to his back-seat man, "if you're for it, let's go." And off they went northbound.

Shortly after the jet had passed over the Ohio River, Don suddenly found those glaring red lights had popped on, identifying one of the engines as being on fire. "My God," Don thought, "I don't wanta bail out of this bird." He quickly shut off the fuel to that engine. After what seemed to be a rather lengthy and nervous period of time, the lights went out. Grateful for that, Don reported being inbound to his airport, explaining he had shut one engine down because of a fire that now appeared to be out. As he began his descent into the Columbus area, he was asked by the tower if he wanted the crash crew to be standing by for his landing. Don thought it wouldn't hurt, and okayed that idea.

Once he reached the airport and entered the traffic pattern, Don learned there was a strong crosswind. Had he been so lucky as to have both engines running, he wouldn't have been concerned, but because he only had the one engine going, Don didn't care for the possible problem the crosswind could become.

Once on the final landing approach and immediately prior to touching the runway, Don did the usual thing and retarded the engine's throttle. With that, the hydraulically powered flight control system suddenly froze! *Don knew what that meant and yelled to his rear-seat man to eject! The uncontrollable aircraft slammed into the ground and bounced!* In the split second it took the plane to reach the apex of the bounce, the man in the back had ejected.

By design, Don's seat would take him out of the aircraft less than a second later. It did so, but *not with the correct trajectory!.. not as planned! The unmanageable aircraft's right wing dropped to a sharp 30 degree angle and struck the earth just as Don and his chair left the disabled machine!*

His seat was then catapulted into an attitude the engineers might call "outside of the design envelope" and headed horizontally down the runway! Don was still strapped in; his 'chute trying to blossom and pull him clear, but it was too late! *Don and the chair had already struck the ground! Don could see what was coming and had thought: "I'm gonna need help on this one.. I'm gonna hit hard!!*

"After I made the first bounce, the seat and I parted company," said Don. "As the 'chute started to open fully, the guys in the control tower saw me tumbling along the ground like a bowling ball.. the movies taken indicated I was rolling at something over 100 miles an hour! Amazingly I never lost consciousness and came to a stop sitting upright. But was I ever bunged up!"

Don's right leg from the knee down was sticking out at a 90 degree angle to the right; the left leg was straight but below the knee it was rotated sharply to his left. He discovered he couldn't move his left arm, but about then the crash crew arrived and told him not to worry about it.. "we'll hit you with some morphine." They did, and the next thing he recalled was awakening in the nearest hospital. The medics later discovered his arm had been broken in three places between the wrist and the elbow. His knees were ruined; every other part of him battered and bruised.

Don was fortunate in becoming a patient of Dr. Paul Miller, then the top orthopedic physician at Ohio State University.

"He put a rod in my left arm and strung the bones like Indian beads. There were countless other surgeries, as well, and about eight weeks later I was shipped west to the San Diego Naval Hospital. I think I've lost track of how many surgeries were performed." *(Ed. note: somewhere between 24 and 30 is Don's best estimate.)*

Obviously, Don, long since retired, has recovered. He may be just short of being a mechanical man but is in such great shape he plays six rounds of golf a week and will often jump at the chance to play seven. He received so much attention from one surgeon, Don ended up becoming his golfing buddy.

By the way, for you green-course hackers, in April '96, Don shot three consecutive 88's.

About flying.. Don says: "If they gave me a chance, I'd be right back in the cockpit of a plane like that."

Frankly, if there ever was "a next time," I believe he would rather exit in the more conventional manner.

While a few of us love the excitement unusual situations can create, most of us are really creatures of a conventional life style.. hoping we can count on rather habitual patterns. Like the usual great weather one finds in Hawaii or the Fall colors doing their big show when we plan to be in the northern latitudes.

But, since nothing in Mother Nature's bag is ever a surety, pilots in years gone by never considered the weatherman's predictions to be anything more "than his best effort" He or she was commonly referred to as the "weather guesser." For long range flights we didn't expect any guarantees. Conditions may have appeared to be excellent at takeoff, but it paid to lend a keen ear to the radio for weather updates as the flight progressed.

Of course weather conditions can be of serious concern anywhere, but flying over the livable continents versus trips over oceanic routes gave flight crews a stronger sense of security.

"Why?" The Atlantic and Pacific Oceans had a scarcity of airports. Naturally, there being darned few islands and even fewer airfields, those latter areas had a great lack of weather reporting stations. Some were separated by as much as two thousand miles—nothing in between.

And in those days who knew what a weather satellite *was,* let alone know what it could produce? Pictures from *space?* Hah! Result: Who could really know what weather lay waiting beyond the horizon?

In the era of the fifties, pilots then were little different from those of today. They gave careful consideration to whatever weather information was available. Pilots applied what they knew or what might be expected, carefully planning *what* they would do *when* (as pilots still do today.)

If they were flying to Wake Island in the mid-Pacific, it was basically a station where weather was little worse than that in Hawaii. Normally, nothing to "sweat" about. If they should arrive at Wake during a period of inclement weather, the aircraft always carried at least two hours of extra fuel just to permit a doubtful pilot time to make up his mind as to *when* he was ready to land at that airfield. There was no other. It was routine. No plane had yet been built that could safely carry enough extra fuel to let the pilot take a brief look at conditions at Wake and then depart for some other airfield.

You realize this is all leading up to a story, don't you?

It began at Hickam Air Force Base in Hawaii on September 14, 1952. The USAF flight crew was in preparation for an extended flight to Tokyo in a Boeing-built C-97, the Air Force version of what was then the newest, most luxurious airliner, the "Stratocruiser." Flying with extra crew members, it would be possible for the Military Air Transport Service aircraft to make a refueling stop at Wake about midnight and then continue on to Haneda Airport in Japan. The total anticipated "on duty" time to Tokyo would exceed twenty hours. (One gives a great deal of thought to a flight of that length!)

As usual, briefing officers in Hawaii supplied the flight crew with every bit of information relative to their mission. Naturally, this included the weather forecast along their route; over Wake Island; what to expect in Japan; even the latest weather at the few islands north and south en route to Wake.

"At Wake Island," said the weather guesser, "you can expect a slight tropical disturbance in the area. You might encounter cloud tops at your flight level.. possibly with a little turbulence. If it was daylight you could probably pick your way around them."

"And it wasn't going to be daylight," thought the pilots.

At the time of the briefing, the wind conditions at Wake were apparently so negligible, no one even recalled the subject being mentioned.

Two hours before reaching Wake, the weather was all the briefing officer had promised. "We were flying through the tops of cumulus clouds and encountering moderate turbulence," volunteered the author's friend Ron. "Within an hour or so we contacted Wake Island for landing instructions, only to learn a 35 mile-per-hour wind was blowing directly *across* the only runway!" A most unusual occurrence at the island and not a favorable situation in daylight or darkness. Obviously the weather was deteriorating. "Everyone agreed it was best to land NOW."

The most experienced pilot aboard took on the task. The stiff crosswind required every bit of his skill. Even so, the landing was so severe, one tire of the two on each main landing gear blew with a noticeable explosion. Because airliners don't carry spare tires, the prognosis for continuing the flight to Japan looked grim.

"Maybe we can borrow two from the Pan Am people," was a suggestion from the crew.

Since Pan Am was under contract to service all transiting MATS aircraft, the idea was fine—up until the time the USAF aircraft commander learned Pan Am had just one tire that would fit the now disabled C-97. The trip to Nippon was indefinitely stalled.

By then, Pan Am operations personnel had determined from their own weather observations we could expect winds of perhaps 60 miles per hour. If that happened, Pan Am wanted some of the USAF flight crew to go aboard the parked aircraft. They would, in effect, be ready to keep the C-97 wedded to the ground by literally "flying" the plane into the face of the expected winds, just in case the big blow became stronger. The aircraft commander and two flight engineers volunteered for that assignment—IF the wind became stronger.

Should this "slight tropical disturbance" become even more forceful, the aircraft, through Mother Nature's help, would still try to "go airborne" just as it does when it reaches flying speed on the takeoff roll. In essence, the fierce wind could make the plane fly even without power! The plane would need a pilot—and possibly its engines running—to literally force the machine to remain on the ground!

Meanwhile, the entire crew and its few passengers were bedded down in a Quonset hut (typical World War II structures designed for quick construction and durability against strong winds.)

At 4:00 a.m. the wind had become stronger and the aircraft standby crew was awakened and driven through the increasing wind to the shivering C-97.

Because of the storm, the remainder of the crew had failed to find sleep. Near daybreak, the copilot finally got up and began getting dressed, when SSSSZZZAP!..off went a portion of the hut's roof! That incident jarred everyone else into action; they hurriedly dressed and fled to the dining hall, a larger Quonset hut.

Soon the howling wind began screaming in greater intensity. By 10 a.m. the heavy hurricane strength wind was laced with pelting rain, and even the huge, extra strong Quonset was beginning to shake, rattle and create anxiety. Until then the occupants of that dining hall had previously been concerned about their obviously endangered fellow flight crewmembers isolated in the stricken aircraft.

Suddenly, in an explosive-like blast, the entire roof peeled away! Now, the seemingly secure people in the big Quonset had their own survival problems!

Ron remembers diving beneath the nearest table into six inches of water as the roof simply disappeared into the unknown! In the immediate vicinity there were only two safe havens on that side of the island—two 'walk-in' refrigerators. Every person in the Quonset struggled against whirling winds and rain to reach the protection the reefers could provide! It was, of course, a chilling reception, and one that lasted almost five hours. They were later to learn the wind speed had peaked near noon at 120-130 mph! "Slight tropical disturbance" indeed! The only above ground structure remaining on the island was the welding shop; just another Quonset hut, but one welded together by the station's welder during his free time.

In time, everyone at Wake learned what had caused their peril. It was a typhoon officially named Olive. "But," as Ron was quick to point out, "Olive certainly was no lady!"

The plane? Oh, it weathered the storm. The watchdog flight crew aboard during the height of the storm may have been scared silly, but they kept the C-97 from disaster. And, although thoroughly salt-encrusted by wind-blown seawater, it eventually acquired the two needed tires and was flown back to Hickam AFB for nearly a month-long removal of the salt corrosion.

Ron said his later excursions into the weather section of Hickam's flight operations seemed to cause a disappearance of the weather guesser. "Probably afraid I would embarrass him by asking if he had anymore of those 'slight tropical disturbances' somewhere."

Talk about survivors, here's a story for you—thanks to the saving grace of God and a helicopter.

Almost from the start, helicopters have demonstrated some outstanding capabilities. One was saving lives.

Most of us fail to realize "choppers," as many people call them, involve principals of flight quite different from those used by the more conventional fixed-wing aircraft. The helicopter does so many things no other aerial vehicle can do.

"Wait," says one fellow the author knows, "I *know* what it can do. Just tell the story."

He doesn't want its history; how it was made, or all the things it can do. He just thanks God that whirligig was there when nothing else could do the job! Anyone who has had an emergency helicopter pickup feels pretty much the same. Forget the facts. They just *love* the chopper.

The 'copter came along in the nick of time, at least for those fighting in the Korean War. That was the "police-action" which began in 1950, when many nations joined together to aid in the defense of South Korea. It's where this story begins. A story of a nonsmoker in battle—and his battle to remain a non-smoker.

If that confuses you, don't give up. We'll get to it.

The author's friend was an Army man, one just old enough to get caught up in the Korean action. All during his younger years he was tempted to become a smoker. Sure.. "everyone else" was lighting up. It didn't keep them from making the varsity football team. Their growth never seemed to be limited. No one had hacking coughs. All they got was a bad time from their parents. Still, this youngster didn't succumb to that nicotine habit, even after he joined the Army.

He soon became deeply involved in the business of war. It was, like all wars, a dirty one. He was in the front lines. The disadvantages made him a believer in General Sherman's historic statement: "War is hell!" Not just from the mud; the snow; the chill winds, the lousy food and the infrequent arrival of mail, it was the presence of a mass of men seemingly all shooting at him!

His unit was in close contact with powerful enemy forces when he was hit. Badly hit. He was down, momentarily unsure of anything but the immediate shock of the impact of the shells that had sent him crashing to the ground. Time had little meaning and his first realization of the grievousness of his wounds came later because of the pain emanating from several points in his ravaged body.

He tried to take stock of his condition. Blood from a frightful shoulder wound oozed across a cold, barely breathing chest. More pain streamed up from his legs; blood literally draining over both; one so badly torn it appeared to be "on backwards." He knew this could be "it" for him.

He had visions of the enemy still being present on the battlefield, an enemy nearly surrounding his position. His brain wasn't functioning at its best, but he was aware his enemy didn't relish taking prisoners unless they were likely to gain valuable military intelligence. If that situation existed, they were capable of torture.

Realizing his wounds were severe—possibly mortal—the desperate soldier vowed not to be further hurt by capture. He fumbled for one of his remaining fragmentation grenades and holding it in one hand, managed to pull the safety pin. Then he struggled to retain his hold on the now hazardous weapon while moving that hand beneath his body. An enemy soldier who might try to capture him would never live to tell of the effort!

Then a miracle! Dangerously close to losing consciousness, he heard the unmistakable voice of an American:

"Hey.. over here! Looks like he's alive!"

At the arrival of the Army medics he became more alert; also more aware of the terrible pain. Yet he doesn't recall warning the stretcher bearers about the armed grenade hidden beneath him. He must have, for they carefully removed the death-dealing hazard from the scene.

To diminish the agony his saviors gave him several hits of morphine, then carried him perhaps a half-mile to a waiting evacuation helicopter.

Still partially conscious, his brain nearly detached from reality, the injured man was strapped into a stretcher lashed to the 'copter's landing skids. He vaguely remembers riding outside in the wind, and in his ethereal state, he fuzzily enjoyed his first flight in a chopper. Below him, mountains; green rice paddies and a relatively peaceful, detached scene. In his hazy condition, he was ecstatic. The ride was outstanding!

As the 'copter descended over the emergency medical facility the soldier was still conscious, though physically immobile. Amidst the arrival of other 'copters, time passed. Here he was, a stretcher case and no one had rushed to deliver him to the MASH unit's tent. Standard procedure was stretchers first; walking wounded next.

"How come??.. there go the *walking wounded!* Do these guys think it's too late for me?.. that I've had it? Well, not if you got me this far, buddy-boys!"

He tried to whistle, but it proved impossible in his condition. He tried singing.. or thought it was singing. "Probably more like moaning," he admits. But it worked!

"Hey!" he heard, "this guy's alive!"

"Wow!" said another, "Give him a smoke.. light it for him for God's sake! There.. now, let's get him inside."

"HEY!.. He's *CHOKING!* It's the *cigarette!*"

"Yeah, the cigarette. Get it outta there!"

The battered G.I. had heard of deaths by "friendly fire," but friendly *cigarettes?*

He still has never learned to smoke.

Out of all the people in the whole world, being the first person to become the leading light during a momentous occasion; to do something no one else has done, is memorable if to no one but the person who accomplishes the feat. Of course some events are more daring; more newsworthy and the public remembers those individuals.

Charles Lindbergh is an example. In 1927 he became the first person to fly solo, nonstop, from New York to Paris; Amelia Earhart was the first woman to fly solo across the Atlantic, etc.

But who recalls the first pilot to land on the big U. S. Air Force base on the island of Guam?

"Who cares? That happened in 1944."

Actually, here in 1996, no one but the fellow who did it gives a darn. But at the time, it was an Army Air Force base (technically still under construction) scheduled to be "home port" for a fleet of B-29 bombers. The runways were completed, but some of the finishing touches were just being cleaned up, then everything would be ready for an official opening of the base.

The Navy SeaBees—a collection of topnotch construction workers in civilian life—were on Guam helping the Army Air Force build the airfield.

One of those gallant SeaBees who had plugged away at creating the new field had a brother. Not just any brother, this one was right on the same island, but in a separate branch of the service. (In a battle area that covered the entire Pacific Ocean, being able to join hands with a brother was worth a celebration all by itself.)

"Hey," said this brother, "hitch a ride and come over and see me. I'm only six or eight miles away."

And the SeaBee brother managed to do that a few days before his duties at the new airfield would be done. They had a good get together and in time the SeaBee was due to hustle himself back to that new airfield.

The SeaBee's brother turned out to be a pilot, and one that suggested: "Why don't I try to bum an airplane and fly you back?"

Naturally the SeaBee had hoped he could someday get his brother to give him an airplane ride, but to have the brother fly him back; to land at what had temporarily become the SeaBee's "home base," that would be something special!

The two brothers acquired a dive bomber for their "SeaBee delivery flight." They buckled themselves in; took off; flew around doing a bit of sightseeing, then came in and landed at the spanking new airfield. No control tower operating; no clearance, just a long, wide, unused runway.

By the way.. that plane landing on the new base was a Navy plane. And the SeaBee's brother was a Navy pilot, and only a young ensign, at that. Here he was, the very first man to put an airplane onto what looked like the newest and longest runway in the world!

But you know politics.. opening a brand new major airfield is deserving of some commemoration; some pomp and ceremony. That kind of excitement brings on matters of protocol.. who should be invited, etc. Even in the middle of a war, the Army Air Force "brass" was taking care of all those big issues. They had scheduled their general to be the pilot making the very first landing.. leaving the first tire marks on a new runway.

Obviously, it didn't work out quite that way.

Have to tell ya'.. that ensign's activity didn't go over so well with a flock of high-ranking Army Air Force officers. If it had been Admiral Nimitz aboard that aircraft, those officers wouldn't have said "boo." But an *ensign?* It rankled them more than somewhat.

Nobody could blame the work-a-day SeaBee. He didn't have the inside word on who was scheduled to make the first landing on the new field. How could he?.. he was a Navyman, a man not privy to the important details of protocol involving "the Army brass." It's likely he never gave it a thought. The same holds true for his brother.. the pilot.. the young ensign.

Yep, that youthful Naval Aviator left a big bunch of Army men quite irritated.

Of course that was in 1944 and the ensign—if he didn't receive immediate orders to the more active war zone, and if he is still alive— can keep asking any of his numerous grandchildren if they ever heard about the time he had a general mad at him. He'd probably love to tell it again.

Naturally, the Navy also has their list of firsts. Like the Army and the Air Force, the Navy has some people of note who usually get the chance to get on "the" list for important events—such as the very first landing on a new aircraft carrier as the ship enters service.

In the decade of the forties there was this ship the USS Wright, a small carrier. It was what most of us called a "baby carrier." Not big enough to handle a full carrier air group—(four to five combat squadrons)—and was used, together with its rather small air group, to go out and hunt down submarines.

My friend, Bill Davis, was a lieutenant (junior grade) doing his flying chores in a rather large piston-engine aircraft which the Navy called an AD-3W, the "Skyraider." Bill's plane was equipped with a radar so large it made the aircraft look like a pregnant guppy.

With the carrier at sea off the Virginia coast, Bill and his guppy were launched to make a submarine search. Not too long after the flight got airborne, Bill was quick to notice the cockpit began filling with smoke—the kind of smoke that smells and tells: "We have an electrical fire." Even if Bill did have any fire-fighting equipment, he didn't have time to use it because he was the guy flyin' the aircraft. ("Besides," he said, "I really didn't know what-was-burning-where. All I could see was smoke.")

So, like a good lad who has some brains, Bill reasoned the best place for him was back on that carrier—*pronto!* Of course, all that smoke could easily have caused Bill to put the guppy in the ocean and no one would have blamed him for ditching.

Bill said, jokingly, "I know better than to try extinguishing an electrical fire with water!" As it turned out, the carrier wasn't all that far away, so his first idea was by far his best choice. He did, however, turn off every bit of electronics and electrical gear but the radio, hoping the fire would go out once he had eliminated the spark that caused it in the first place.

While he was quickly accelerating his guppy to its best speed, he was calling the ship's radio and requesting an emergency landing. The ship gave him no argument on his request and readied the deck for his landing.

"Truly," he said, "I wanted to save the government's airplane because I knew it was valuable, but I was also thinking about how valuable my backside was—at least to me."

Bill picked up the ship rapidly; received his clearance to land; found the landing signals officer waving his "paddles" to guide the plane into its proper position, and Bill happily thumped the wheels on the carrier's deck. The crash crew was right by his side as he hopped nimbly out the of the smokey aircraft, safe and sound.

It didn't take long for Bill to start receiving congratulations from any number of the carrier's crew. In the haze of excitement over his brush with the Grim Reaper, it took Bill sometime to realize: "These guys weren't laying on the congratulations because I got back safely. I had just made the 17,000th landing on the old Wright!"

Ed. Note: On carriers, every thousandth landing is also considered an event and a suitable ceremony is made over the pilot who makes the landing.

Of course, a ceremony *had* already been planned—but not for Bill Davis. The carrier's skipper had helped plan it for Bill's big boss, the commander of his air group, a flier keyed to make that landing and accept the appropriate honors.

Bill wasn't quite sure how the commander took it, but:

"Personally," said Bill, "I didn't feel too badly about it."

Have you ever noticed that sometimes the bright green of money overpowers any concern over what otherwise would be a dangerous situation? As witness the following:

Being an aviation "nut" is one thing. Being a souvenir hunter is another. The two activities are sometimes compatible. When they are, you've found a man like the daredevil folks remember up in central California.

They called him Gary. As a young man he loved the concept of flying and had barely learned the art when his primary interest soon turned to the retrieval of old aircraft from hiding places in "wherever."

Gary's first old bird was a 1939 era Lockheed Lodestar, a twin-engine airliner whose best service was with the almost forgotten National Airlines in the southeast corner of the United States. Gary claims to have purchased that plane about 30 years ago through a government auction of confiscated equipment.

At the time, Gary wasn't what you'd call an experienced pilot in *any* type of plane. He was still quite young and certainly had never flown a Lodestar. But the moment the government disposed of the plane, it was relieved of having to pay the airfield operator any further storage charges. Since Gary had legal title to the aircraft, his choice was pay rent or fly it away.

Gary had used virtually every dollar he could scrape together just to buy the plane and a new set of sparkplugs for each engine. No way he could pay rent or hire an experienced pilot.

He flew the Lodestar.

Through the years Gary hunted down ancient aircraft in every segment of the western hemisphere. Some weren't even flyable, like the scrapped amphibian aircraft he brought out of the Alaskan bush country; an old World War II Navy fighter out of the cold waters of Seattle's Lake Washington, and a mid-thirties era Army bomber found in Hawaii.

He also discovered a flyable ex-Navy PBY seaplane in Canada; another in Hawaii; a four-engine Douglas DC6 airliner in Arizona and a former Air Force light bomber stranded in a Kansas cornfield with a cracked wing spar.

"No one in his right mind would fly that plane out of a cornfield," said Gary, but after patching up the spar with long bars of titanium, he claims to have done so.

Gary didn't do all that hazardous work for love. He always looked upon it as a profit-making business. He would fix up his acquisitions either for further flying by the buyer or for aircraft displays in museums around the nation. Those few which logically couldn't become a financial success, he traded off for some other junker he thought would be profitable.

In the 1980's Gary managed to acquire a twin-engine World War II Navy patrol bomber called a PV2, a more powerful, more advanced design built around the basic plans of Gary's first plane, the Lodestar.

Gary learned the Navy air museum people in Pensacola, Florida, were always on the lookout for former Navy planes not already in their custody. He made a deal to sell the museum his PV2. There was one major stipulation: They weren't coming to him for it; he was obligated to deliver it.

And delivery of a plane as ancient as the PV2 was where Gary was going to learn what 'hazardous' really meant.

He spruced up the aircraft as best he could, replicating the original paint job. Some parts of the plane didn't work as the Lockheed engineers had planned, but no matter, Gary decided, his trip east from California would be the PV's last flight.

As in almost every one of Gary's acquisitions, having no real flying experience in the make and model never stopped him from strapping himself in and heading out.. He managed to find a young, untested guy as his copilot for the ancient PV's flight to the Navy's Sherman Field, Pensacola.

The 2,200 mile trip east was going well until they were over Arkansas. Suddenly, the strong smell of fuel invaded the cockpit. It's a situation every pilot knows is a highly dangerous condition and one that makes every crewman sweat. His plane had literally been converted into a flying bomb! The slightest spark and one thunderous blast would fill the atmosphere with flame!

For fear of explosion, Gary instantly shut down everything that was electrically powered, including the radios. The copilot went aft to scout out the problem. He quickly returned to report the bomb bay was half filled with gas. It was clear one of the plane's original synthetic rubber fuel tanks had ruptured.

Gary knew if the plane landed *anywhere,* it would never make another takeoff, for the ruptured tank was irreplaceable. His contract called for delivery. What to do? Be safe and land soonest?.. or press on?

Gary made a financial decision. Despite a severe shortage of fuel; 400 miles to go and no radio he *had* to make it!

Eventually the weary PV arrived at Sherman Field only to find five Navy jet fighters practicing touch-and-go landings. One after another they crowded each other's tail fins making a continuous flow of landings and takeoffs.

If the people manning the control tower tried to call him, Gary didn't know. They were undoubtedly watching "that old clunker circling the field," but offered no volunteer help with their flashing red and green signal light.

Even without a usable gas gauge he knew his fuel supply to be dangerously low. He had little choice. Find an opening—or make one—in that traffic pattern of jet fighters. Gary selected a narrow opening. He decided it was his only chance and squeezed the PV into the landing pattern.

Gary brought his plane in for its final landing, without the tower's clearance. Naturally, that brought down the wrath of the base operations people, and a large number of anxious security personnel "greeted" the PV immediately after it left the runway.

Meanwhile Gary's only thought was in getting the hell out of that machine to breathe fresh air again.

Gary kept his part of the bargain; presumably he got paid. The fractured PV2, now a significant addition to the Navy's air museum, has renewed its acquaintance with a number of veterans who once knew the old bird well.

Gary? He's still doing his thing.. chasing after planes built before he was born.

And Gary would give his left arm and three toes to find one of the airplanes in the following story.

One of the rarest aircraft ever found in the air, yet it was a designated Navy fighter-type of the 1930's era, long after the Navy had developed their force of aircraft carriers and fighter squadrons.

If you know or remember anything about Navy carrier planes, you are aware they all have a hook under the tail of the aircraft. A hook the pilot lowers when he wants his tailhook to snag one of the cables lying across the carrier's flight deck, bringing the plane to a very rapid stop.

The "Sparrowhawk" also had a hook—on the *top* of the aircraft. "On *top?*"

Yep. Still had wheels on the underside like almost every other aircraft, but the "Sparrowhawk" was the only production Navy fighter *not* designed to land aboard an aircraft carrier.

"So.. why the hook on top? For clouds?"

Nothing quite that exotic, but you're close. It hooked up on something nearly as big as a cloud. In fact, it is often remembered as the "aluminum cloud." It was a Navy dirigible. Something like the Goodyear blimp, only twenty times its size, and long out of favor with people in the aeronautics field.

Dirigibles had a metal framework beneath the skin of the craft. Within the skin were many separate cells filled with helium. Blimps differ in that they aren't built with the framework. Let all the helium out of a blimp and it would just look like a flattened hot air balloon. Not so the dirigible. Anyhow, they're old hat.. proved to be impractical for several reasons.

Nonetheless, there were two such gas-filled monsters in the United States Navy in the first half of the 1930's. Each of them could lower a trapeze below the hull. The little "Sparrowhawk" would fly up underneath the dirigible and snag its hook on a trapeze. Result: The trapeze; the "Sparrowhawk" and its pilot were all hoisted up into the belly of the airship.

Those small fighters were built as biplanes and their primary purpose was scouting and/or airborne defense against any enemy planes. Only a small number were assigned to each of the Navy dirigibles, hence only a dozen or so were ever built.

The entire concept was gutsy. A skyborne giant, floating majestically as the largest target an enemy flock of vultures could ever hope to find. High above this silver-colored "cloud" would be two "Sparrowhawks" circling cautiously eyeing the sky around them for any sign of predators. Deep in the "cloud," the mother craft, two other "Sparrowhawks" were haltered by their human pilots; secured to the trapeze and swung into place below the spacious "flying hawks' nest." Quickly they are successively dropped free of the slow moving mother craft and rapidly wheel up and around it climbing skyward to meet with their twin combatants. Their haven, meanwhile, disguises its presence by slipping to a higher altitude and burying itself unseen in one of nature's original clouds.

High above in the clear open sky the "Sparrowhawks" continue their vigil of surveillance and protection against the predators. And the fearsome vultures are chased away or discouraged by their inability to find what would have been their primary 'kill' of the week.

Far-fetched?? Perhaps it was, but no one ever learned that it couldn't have happened. While the defensive scenario was set more or less in that fashion, the "aluminum clouds" were short-lived, each coming down at sea. One in the Atlantic crashed with great loss of life; the other settled rather slowly into the Pacific following loss of both rudder control and the unexplained release of too much helium.

And virtually all of the small, beautiful, and highly maneuverable "Sparrowhawks" clung tightly to their mother craft—even in death.

Curtiss-built U.S. Navy F9C ("Sparrowhawk") was the company's last fighter plane accepted by the U. S. Navy. The trapeze, hung below the plane's "mother" carrier-- one of two lighter-than-air dirigibles--captured the Sparrowhawk's hook and hoisted its cargo into the belly of the airship. In recovering the small fighter, the airship had to reach an airspeed faster than the F9C's stall speed.

The heroes of Britain fought through 1940-42 against overwhelming odds while fighting back waves of German aircraft during the "Battle of Britain." A vast majority of those pilots used the famous "Spitfire,"(above) an aircraft to ultimately become the primary English fighter over its earlier competition, the Hawker "Hurricane."

One of the world's great fighter planes of World War II was the North American Aircraft Company's P-51 "Mustang." Still sought after today for its speed, world class racing pilots seek more Mustangs than any other propeller-driven aircraft.

A leading Navy/Marine fighter type of WW II and the late forties was the F4U "Corsair." Well used during a crucial battle period within the So. Pacific, USMC units virtually intimidated enemy forces by using the F4U as both a fighter and a ground support attack aircraft. Enemy air force units easily identified it in the air by its unusual inverted gull wing, while their ground forces simply identified it: "Whistling Death."

While the well-known U.S. built Boeing B-17 was used extensively in both the relatively close confines of the European combat zone and the more expansive areas of the So. Pacific, history records it as being one of the major reasons why the Allied forces in WW II were able to overpower German military productivity.

SOME PEOPLE GET THE WORD

Wild or humorous tales exist in every facet of life, even safetyminded aviation. But can we find something funny in a weatherguesser's existence?

You bet.

Many of you may know the airline captain doesn't just climb aboard an aircraft without a considerable degree of help from a supporting staff. A part of that group is the weatherman. In the captain's primary support force are dispatchers, people knowledgeable in the study of weather.

Many dispatchers started their life's work by gathering weather information. This one fellow began his as a youngster in the Navy. He loved to tell this story on himself, and always got a big laugh when he did so: His first 'solo' adventure involving a weather balloon.

These balloons, somewhat larger than the toys we loved as kids, were filled with helium. Tied to them were special instruments, scheduled to be launched every six hours by each of the official weather stations around the nation. Watching the balloon disappear into the clouds was the weatherman's idea of learning the height of the cloud base above the airport, an important issue to flyers. It still is today.

The whole operation was a one-man job and simply blowing up a balloon and eyeballing its flight wasn't enough. Because timing its rise into the cloud layer was most important, knowing the precise weight of the balloon and its instruments was also important. The weatherman knew it took the balloon so many seconds to reach 1,000 feet... so many more to reach 2,000, etc. Timing was accomplished with a stopwatch. If the balloon disappeared in 45 seconds, he could calculate just how high the bottom layer of cloud cover was above the ground.

And now we come to the real good part of our story.

When it was "balloon releasing time" it was usually done from the highest available part of the building. In this particular story it was from a balcony. The person involved in this one-man job held the balloon in one hand, the stopwatch in the other.

This young novice "weather-guesser" was filled with anxiety for his first go with this balloon project. Nervous as he was, hand-eye coordination got the better of him. With the watch ready in one hand; the balloon all set to fly in the other, the Navyman let go...

Of the watch!

Could we assume it was a shattering experience on his first watch?

On a day of clouds and low-altitude turbulence in the early winter of '42, Wally, future captain, hadn't quite reached his level of aviation maturity. In fact, he had barely earned his commercial license when he joined his airline in November, 1941.

Flying out of Hilo, Hawaii, under the silent guidance of Gilbert Tefft in the company's only flyable DC3, Wally was at the controls, just under the "soup" in rain showers. Gil, as was his custom in those old days, was reading his newspaper.

Wally didn't appreciate the bumpy skies and found what looked like a hole in the clouds. He proceeded upwards, hoping to get above the weather. But the hole closed in on him. He was trained enough to maintain flight using the cockpit instruments and he went "on the gauges."

At the time Hawaii had no such thing as air traffic control to issue clearance for flight in the clouds. Folks just did it.

Wally kept climbing; every so often looking up at the windshield to see if he had reached the top yet, but he could never see out and he'd quickly go back to use of his flight instruments.

Finally Captain Tefft started feeling the cold of altitude and decided he was chilled enough, it was high time Wally learned a little more about flying.

Gil reached into his bag and pulled out a cloth; stretched himself over to Wally's windshield and wiped away Wally's "clouds."

There was blue sky outside; the DC3 far and away above the weather below them. Gil long ago realized the higher you go, the colder the windows get, and when you bring a cockpit filled with moist, heated air from sea level into the drier, chillier temperature of altitude, the windows all fog up.

There are many tales about Gil Tefft and his life in the Hawaiian Islands, most of them much more meaningful.

Gil was a flier who opted out of the old Army Air Corps in 1930 to come fly with a small airline just starting to make history in the Hawaiian Islands.

Where Gil had spent the last part of his Army career, trees, flowers and green hills weren't common parts of the landscape. Hawaii, of course, had an abundant supply. From his early Army flying days in Hawaii he knew what life in the islands was like. He must have missed those natural items of beauty, for he was always immensely grateful he had been invited to fly for Inter-Island Airways.

Remember the story about America's Johnny Appleseed? Walked the countryside eating apples?.. then fostered the growth of apple trees by flinging the seeds along the roadway? He didn't have anything on Captain Gil Tefft. Both were active in contributing to the nurturing of new life—plant life.

Gil just did his in a more modern style. He didn't walk the pathways of the countryside, he flew.

By 1935, his spare time in the islands was being well spent putting his own mark on the growing of orchids. He began raising all of the better known hybrids, the orchids girls use for corsages and the vandas used for making Hawaiian leis. He soon learned most everything there was to know about orchids, and he had his own beliefs on how they would grow best.

He figured there was probably no better place for orchids to grow than in the heavy rain forest so common to much of Hawaii's largest island. And before long Gil took to carrying vials filled with water and small orchid slips, and on sunny days inbound to Hilo he would angle his plane over the forest areas, open the cockpit window, and empty the vials of different orchid varieties—cattleyas, dendrobriums and the like.

In time Gil learned even more about how orchids grew and decided all he needed to do was carry a packet of seed pods. When he reached the desired area, with the seeds in his hand, he'd just slide open the cockpit window; the wind whistling by sucked the seeds right out into the plane's slipstream.

Over time, local people who hunted in the forest lands above the Hamakua-to-Hilo coastline began spotting these big hybrid orchids growing where only wild orchids had ever been seen before.

Gil never had much to say about his part in the orchid seeding program, but eventually the story came out in the newspaper, referring to Gil as the Johnny Appleseed of the orchid world.

A reporter from the paper asked him how well he thought his seeding effort would do.

"Fine," said Gil, "the less care you give an orchid the better." Gil added he didn't believe orchids should be coddled.

When that statement came out in the paper, one of his previous copilots said:

"I think you'll find he feels the same way about copilots. And I believe he'd like to drop some of them out the window, too."

From that last observation you can probably gather that Gil wasn't always every copilot's choice as "most lovable captain of the month."

Captain Tefft's rather consistent pattern on each of his flights was to make the takeoff; reach an altitude of approximately 1,000 feet, then turn to his copilot and point to the copilot's flight controls. Gil would then light up his standard cigar and start reading the daily paper. He read until the destination airport appeared below, thereupon promptly take over the controls and land.

But one former pilot the author knows seemed to have an inherent ability to get the best out of his flights with Gil. This fellow Ted had a flair for good public relations; knew what brand of cigar Gil smoked flight after flight, and tried to improve his captain's happiness level each day by offering him that favorite cigar.

The result: Ted got plenty of time at the controls; even the privilege of making a few landings and takeoffs.

Retired Captain P. R. M. Fowler recently told this story about himself and the late Captain Horace Pope.

In all airlines the dispatcher and the captain jointly sign a flight clearance. That piece of paper has all the pertinent facts written or printed on it, or attached thereto. In those days the dispatch form at Hawaiian Airlines was simple and relatively brief. Use of check marks, circles or other "quick-fix" ways to tell the pilot where he was supposed to go was standard practice.

On this one particular day, Pete is flying copilot to Horace... They've got a DC3 load of passengers halfway from Honolulu to their destination, Maui. As usual, the copilot is monitoring the company's private radio frequency just in case communication is needed between home base's dispatch office and the aircraft.

Suddenly that radio circuit came alive with a call from Honolulu: "Hawaiian 16.. This is Dispatch. Circle Lanai. Over."

The message received, the DC-3 crew calls a "Roger" back to Dispatch. Both pilots figured orders are orders and Horace changes course a smidgen and heads for the island of Lanai, only a few miles to the right of their original course. "Okay, we'll circle Lanai," says Horace.

Neither of the pilots had any idea which of their passengers had so much clout the company would send a plane out of its way for sightseeing. But, it wasn't their worry. "Circle Lanai."

Once they reached the western shore of Lanai, Horace put the plane in a shallow little turn, keeping the plane just about a mile offshore and high enough for any interested passenger to get a good look at all sides of the 'pineapple' island.

Once that little tour was over, Horace again headed off for nearby Maui. Arriving on the Valley Isle, Horace was asked to give Dispatch a call.

And he did. The first thing Honolulu had to say: "How come you didn't land at Lanai?"

"You didn't circle Lanai on my dispatch release," Horace replied.

There was a long silence on the phone. "That's why we radioed you: *'Circle Lanai.'* We wanted you to **circle** the **name** Lanai on your release so you would know to **land** there."

Communications between us humans—whether written or radioed—obviously hasn't yet become a fool-proof program. It is often plagued by: "Murphy's Law." *If there's a way to louse it up, somebody will do it.*

So it is occasionally between captains and the mechanics. Frequently an aircraft returns to its base and the mechanics discover the captain has placed a 'write up' in the aircraft log book... a complaint which requires a mechanic to fix the problem. The book, by the way, is a critical part of the plane's inventory. In all cases of a captain's "write-up," a written response is necessary regarding the action taken by the maintenance crew. In all cases, it is so important the aircraft is not allowed to fly until that complaint is 'signed off' by the mechanic as having been repaired, replaced or accounted for as being justifiably deferred.

Most of the people who do much flying like to believe the good hand of the Lord supports the plane anytime they get airborne.

And if it isn't the Lord who gets the credit, most folks pass that honor to the pilots.

There may be merit in all that, but....

You talk with aircraft mechanics and they'll tell you all the pilots have to do is "push or pull a few switches and controls, point the airplane up or down, and maybe talk real good over the public address system." They'll tell you the mechanics are the guys who make things work; it's their business to fix the airplanes and assorted parts the "dumb" pilots manage to break.

All things considered, keeping the planes in the air is a full time job for pilots *and* mechanics.. not to mention God and some air traffic controllers.

However, sooner or later pilots in every flight operation will discover the same part of a specific plane's equipment has been consistently written up as a problem. Yet in spite of many captains' "write ups" and repeated repairs or adjustments by mechanics, the gidget or gadget just doesn't do its job when airborne. An investigation of the log book would reveal the same "write up" has been made for every flight, maybe four or five times before. And each time the boys in Maintenance have given this gidget a good try at fixing the problem. Through the plane's log book the mechanics have reported back: "checks out O.K. on the ground."

Captain Howard wrote up a complaint, knowing the mechanics would have to fix the problem. Three or four days later he was assigned the same airplane. He read through the log book as he was obligated to do, and found the same complaint had been reported by every captain who'd flown the plane since.

But each time Maintenance had done what they thought was necessary and 'signed off' the book: "it checks out O.K. on the ground."

Howard could've done what one captain did: "If the goddamned thing always checks out O.K. on the ground, maybe that's where they ought to leave it."

Howard isn't too good at that kind of language, but he either had a bad day, or he felt like it was time to fluster the mechanics a bit. When he returned from this last flight, he wrote up the same complaint one more time, but now he added:

"Hebrews 13:8." Nothing else. Just Hebrews 13:8.

Hebrews 13:8 got 'em! The night maintenance crew tried to do their job, but they couldn't fathom why the reference to Hebrews 13:8. They couldn't ignore it, for everything a captain writes in the log in terms of a complaint has to be acknowledged by the maintenance people.

At 4:00 a.m. the dispatcher, calls Howard on the phone and apologizes all over the place for having to wake him, but they just can't figure out what Hebrews 13:8 means. The dispatcher added: "Until the maintenance people know and can respond, that airplane won't go any place!"

Howard says: "Did you show 'em a bible?"

"Well no," says the dispatcher, "that's our problem. We don't have one."

"Okay," says Howard, "I'll tell you: Hebrews 13:8 says: `Jesus Christ, the same yesterday, and today, and forever.'"

That bible lesson must have helped the mechanics some—they fixed the problem.

In most airline companies there exists an extensive supply of reading material. Several of the larger books, or manuals, literally become "the bible" to a majority of the company employees. To the pilots there is the big thick aircraft manual covering every piece of equipment on the airplane. To the people in the maintenance shops, each of their specialties—engines, hydraulics, electronics, etc.—has their own lengthy publications documenting every possible part.

Then there are the long, boring, seemingly repetitious examples of the lawyers' skill—labor contracts. And most airline companies work their employees through a union labor contract, pilots included. The contracts mean no long-term employee can be fired without due cause and without being supported by dutifully kept records.

For pilots, none of them become "long-term" employees until they have struggled through a year's probation. Until twelve months go by, they are still called "new hires" and subject to being discharged at the chief pilot's discretion.

Naturally, each of those new hire pilots tries to maintain a squeaky clean attitude and an exemplary behavior pattern for that first year. None want to be out pumping gas at the corner service station next week.

For most new employees, the first year is spent getting to know the job and learning what is expected of them. For pilots, there is more: the government requires they attend ground school classes on the model and type of aircraft they will be flying. Classes filled with hours of study and discussion about how the electrical and hydraulic systems operate; the proper uses of the aircraft emergency procedures, and a host of other applicable information. The classes go on for three or four weeks.

Years back, a group of pilots was attending such a class. All but one were "new hires." That single pilot (we'll call him Bud) had been away on a leave of absence for two or three years. He'd passed through the probation period, and unlike his classmates, he was solidly on the airline's seniority list. But by virtue of FAA rules, Bud had been out of action so long he had to do the schooling bit all over again.

Being a kind of a joker, Bud made the most of his association with the new pilots, none of whom knew Bud's airline status was any different from their own—new hires on the job. And none of them realized Bud knew the ground school instructor well.

Early on in the class, the instructor had been talking away about some good stuff involving the airplane they all were due to fly. Suddenly he turned to Bud and said:

"Now, can you explain to us what I just said?"

"Beats the hell outta me.. I was asleep!" answered Bud.

The instructor didn't say a word.

The shocked members of that class couldn't believe their ears!

When the next coffee break came around, a new hire named Joe sidled up to Bud and says:

"Hey, fella...you'd better watch it. When you're in your first year, you're on probation. You could get your butt fired!"

Bud couldn't miss this chance. He put on his best bug-eyed, scared look and said:

"Hey, man, thanks for tellin' me. Boy, I hope I didn't blow it. I'll watch my step from now on!"

As things worked out with those two gentlemen, Joe eventually flew copilot to Bud and got to know Bud's most notable characteristic—his short fuse about perceived foul-ups in company management. Bud was a lovable kind of guy but there were frequent opportunities for him to lose his cool, ranting and raving over the "dumb, stupid deal they pulled today!" Those blowups could occur at any given time—airborne or wherever.

In essence, nobody in the airline knew when Bud might "fly off the handle" with a gripe or two.

As the years rolled by, Joe was upgraded to the captain's seat and the author had the pleasure of flying copilot to him one beautifully clear day. No traffic in the area; no meaningful amount of radio communications and for a relatively long while, little verbal action between pilots.

Finally, Joe said: "Well, this is my last leg for the day. How about you?"

"Not me.. I've got two more trips."

"Who ya with?" asks Joe.

"Bud."

No comment from Joe.. just silence.

The silence lasted about ten minutes, then suddenly, Joe shed his sun glasses onto the control pedestal in a dramatic manner; slammed the sun shield with one hand; bouncing the other hand against the top of the instrument panel, all the while cursing a blue streak.

Surprised by the sudden outburst, your author asked: "What the hell was that all about?"

Joe turned and smiled. "Just warmin' ya up for Bud."

So... there's often excessive noise inside the aircraft as well as on the outside. Not too often people flying in the larger jet airliners will ever complain of too much noise. However, that isn't always true concerning those people who live or work near or under an airport's flight pattern.

But it's not surprising there are always several residents of any age group who resent "airport noises." They move into the immediate vicinity of large airports and then form indignate neighborhood committees to "do something about the terrible noise" problem.

In that vein, if someone moved an *airport* into close proximity of my house, I'd feel politically correct in squawking about it. But how come people will buy, build or rent under the airport traffic pattern.. then later become ardent anti-noise fans?

It's quite true the booming age of jet engines didn't do much for peace and quiet, at least for those who were living next to the airport. The engines we had during the first 15-20 years did have what might be called an "audio drawback." Even the quieter engines of today haven't satisfied all of the objectors' complaints.

The truism exists: You can't please everybody.

But now we get into the humorous part.

Several years ago a large airport with its resident jets and airlines were being hassled by a citizens' "anti-noise" committee. In defense against the complaints received, an airline representative spent untold hours moving around the airport's perimeter with an instrument that could accurately measure the decibels each time a jet passed overhead or nearby. He carefully recorded his readings.

Soon after, this anti-noise committee scheduled a public meeting, hoping to line up more support for their cause.

The noise-collecting airline man attended. He brought his readings and his decibel meter.

Turns out the chairman of the anti-noise group had spent *beau coup* time involved in aviation and was basically a "self-proclaimed expert" on *anything* having to do with the world of flight. For reasons known only to himself—and perhaps a few exemployers—it seemed he had a "thing" about the local air facility and its tenants.

As the meeting progressed, the airline rep with the decibel meter kept hearing the "expert" loud and clear, and he came up with a thought:

"Yeah," he said to himself, "why don't I?" and turned his meter to 'on.'

The decibel readings he received?

The speaker was louder than the recorded airplanes.

One noisy talker the author knows is louder than the airplanes, too. And here's where we deviate just a bit from the word 'human' in the book's title. We're talking about a parrot, now. A bloody parrot that almost seems to be human.

When anyone starts up a conversation about flying, the author is one who tries to remember who really started this business, those 'naturals' in the world of flight—the birds. And it's amazing how skilled ol' "Henry" is when anybody starts making with the conversation; he can just about keep up with any person you know.

Henry is a beautiful green parrot. A close friend has had him for years. Of course Henry does a precise imitation of his mistress; has an amazingly clear-spoken vocabulary and even sings an operatic aria or two. Because "Henry" is always caged and unable to be seen from the open-air front entrance, he has befuddled callers who have vocally announced themselves at our friend's front door.

It took two weeks after the family's acquisition of a new dog before the hound finally realized Henry was doing most of the dog calling. When the phone rang, Henry insisted on telling the man of the house to answer it.

Once when unwanted solicitors came, they didn't just knock.. they politely uttered a warm and friendly: "Aloha.. is anyone home?" The lady of the house had earlier observed their arrival and ducked out of sight.

Back comes this very gracious response from an unseen corner of the house: "Ahhh-loh-hah.. how are yooey-yooey?"

"Could we speak with you for a moment?" replied one of the visitors.

Again from the depths of the house: "Ah-loh-ha. Hi."

It took a few minutes of such simplified conversation or a few bars from an aria before the solicitors realized the present address was turning into a waste of time, and probably quite unsure of who or what was the opposite party. The visitors, obviously puzzled, departed.

But there is more to Henry. The author once took his birdship under his wing (pun intended) when Henry's mistress and husband were moving. Keeping Henry in a disrupted household was expected to become something of a hardship, so the author volunteered to fly him to the city of his next abode; "parrot-sitting" him until his "parents" could retrieve him.

When the day came for Henry's initial departure, he was placed in a travel cage like those normally used for carrying cats. He was delivered to the airport terminal where the author's plane was due to depart for Henry's new destination. Immediately prior to loading passengers, Henry's temporary cage was placed up front in the small bag and coat locker opposite the DC-9's door.

Until the boarding process began, Henry had been noticeably quiet. As the passengers filed in, he suddenly came alive. He welcomed each and every one—120 in all—with a very loud, but a very feminine and drawn-out: "Hyyyy."

If it had been left up to the entranceway flight attendant, Henry's pass would have been canceled then and there. This pilot wasn't too popular, either.

As long as we're into birds, humor me for another captivating tale about a family of wild pheasants at one of the author's departure airports.

Some weeks following the arrival of the mama bird's little darlings, she felt obligated to have the chicks learn the territory. As the author's jetliner was en route via a perimeter taxiway to the takeoff runway; some 800 feet ahead was the mama pheasant walking; her brood in a close line behind. It was obvious their intent was to cross our DC-9's taxiway. Jay-walking, as it were.

As we let the plane continue to close upon the trespassers, expecting them to break ranks and scatter, they fearlessly kept to their course, the mama pheasant apparently believing "no jet plane has a higher priority than we do." Less than 100 feet to go before we would have terminated their future, we gave up—stopping and waiting until mama and her six chicks waddled casually to the opposite side.

Charles Lindbergh's famous "Spirit of St. Louis" acquired its legendary fame by flying more than 33 ½ non-stop hours New York-Paris in May 1927. The aircraft soon took up residence in the Smithsonian Museum, Washington, DC, while Lindbergh continued to actively further the cause of aeronautical development.

A Magic Carpet.. for 25 years..

And still going strong!

One aircraft known to virtually all peoples on earth is the famed Boeing 747. Built in Everett, Washington, USA, these massive air carrier aircraft have been in service for over a quarter of a century.

Worldly air travel 60 years ago..

Slow, but classy!

Pan American World Airways' Martin M-130 "Clipper" during a layover in Pearl Harbor, Hawaii, on its initial trans-Pacific revenue flight San Francisco-Manila, November 1935. Only three of these aircraft were built. They were the first intercontinental air transports and the direct predecessors to the larger, more sumptuous Boeing 314 clippers developed in the late 1930's.

SEXUAL HARASSMENT? *NAAAH..* NOT US!

It's not hard to believe the world's practical jokers' society includes pilots among its millions of members. And practical jokers in all walks of life find the presence of a newcomer or a rookie a challenge to their imagination.

Looking back into the years, there were more practical jokes aboard aircraft than any person will find in today's world of aviation.

Quite a few of those gags were used to bedevil the poor innocent young ladies airlines hired as stewardesses. Ladies who came with a good formal education but with not much in the way of what the modern age call "street smarts."

Most, if not all, were from families who respected the older traditions of life.. good morals... love and marriage go together, etc. In general, they often had a lot to learn in how to deal with the macho male in what was basically "his" domain. Back then we called the girls "stews." In the DC-3 there was only the one, and obviously dominated by two more experienced males.

One captain's favorite gag was the water trick.

Just prior to landing on a nice smooth day, this pilot would casually saunter aft through the cabin. Perhaps he'd do a little public relations work and mix it up with a few passengers, but in the end he was headed for the water jug way in the rear of the cabin. Once there, he would pour a small paper cup half full.

He couldn't wait, but the water wasn't needed for his refreshment. This pilot had something else in mind and it was important he did it all without being observed. The cup had to be placed very carefully on the narrow edge of an air vent high up on the rear wall of the cabin; his whole plan based on the fact the cup was in a precarious position. If the sky was even slightly bumpy or his control of the aircraft was rough, the trick's surprise would be wasted.

Once our jokester captain had the cup all rigged in its sensitive location, he'd get back to the cockpit in time to ready the plane for landing. Of course before touch down, everybody had to be in their seats, the stewardess included. Once she received her "ready for landing" signal she knew enough to get herself back to her regularly assigned seat in the rear of the cabin.

That seat, (by sheer coincidence) was directly in front of, and immediately below, the well balanced cup of water.

Not even one of Captain Paul's good landings could keep that cup of water from tumbling forward onto the hapless girl's head and shoulders.

Were we guilty of picking on the disproportionate number of females who begain filling aviation jobs? Maybe so. After all, where did all these sexual harassment charges come from? Innuendos?

San Francisco had a female controller or two in those earlier days. One, says a friend, was heard to call a TWA flight and ask: "Is my transmission fuzzy?"

The only response (from wherever): "I don't know, honey. Is it?"

Another call, also from San Francisco told an airborne TWA flight: "Stop right there!"

The captain's answer: "This is an airplane, not a car. I can speed up, slow down or reverse course, but I cannot stop. What do you want me to do?"

When you hear some of these stories about the old days, you must wonder just how much attention pilots gave to the job at hand. Flying, that is.

Today things are different. The speed of modern aircraft, the heavy increase of air traffic, and the complexity of technology existing within the aircraft makes horsing around a very questionable game to play. The Federal Aviation Administration is tough and intolerant of tomfoolery; the airline employee's own company objects to it.

As you've already learned, ragging the rookies in any business is (or was) common; much like sending the new kid in the machine shop for a left handed monkey wrench. Perhaps boredom gave pilots time to think up gags to pull on the brand new flight attendant—in the days before we got so concerned over sexual harassment. Of course each gag involving a new stewardess might end up with the poor girl in tears, overworked, or frustrated—perhaps all three.

But on one such occasion, a neat little stunt backfired and somebody else got overworked.

It was during a multi-stop flight from initial departure down "the line" through three landings at other airports. A new girl making her initial trip in the old DC-3 was fresh-faced and eager to learn.

But the captain recognized her as a "new one" and quite naturally had to brief the young lady on a duty "apparently neglected" during the girl's indoctrination check-out. He had to show her what she should do to place the plane's tailwheel safely in the "down" position. Of course that was just a gag in itself; the tailwheel was *always* down. It was built that way. (The "important" wall switch simply served another, rather minor function.)

The captain instructed her that upon hearing the little bell telling her "We're about to land," she was to hustle herself back to the aft baggage compartment and place the specific wall switch in the down position.

Only then, she was told, would the plane's tailwheel come down.

"Just like we have do up in the cockpit to make the main landing gear come down," he added.

The first three landings all went well. The captain made the "before landing" bell ring and our girl did all the things she was expected to do, including "putting the tail wheel down."

Then came the descent into their destination airport where weather conditions promised to give the pilots a good workout.

On that day it was worse than usual. The wind was a strong crosswind; the rain was a falling flood.. more than the plane's windshield wipers could handle. The clouds had dropped right down to minimum altitude allowable for landing, and the cockpit was just about as wet inside as it was out.

Meanwhile, our ambitious new hire back in the cabin had her hands full trying to keep a few white-knuckled passengers from getting airsick.

At this particular airport, duties like working the radio, paying special attention to the flight instruments, and worrying about the worsening weather took all of the pilots' attention. It was the kind of weather that left no time to even think of "horseplay." In those days there was no radar or instrument landing system to help the pilot find the runway. Both pilots had enough to do just flying the airplane.

Those two pilots weren't too concerned about what was happening back in the cabin. As a matter of fact they were so busy their usual bell signaling "ready to land" was forgotten. And most assuredly they had forgotten the gag—the instruction they had laid on the "stew" earlier.

In any event, the lowering of the main landing gear caused the new "stew" to realize the aircraft was indeed intending to land—and quickly. She knew she wasn't ready; she hadn't even checked the passengers' seat belts. She was up front in the cabin unable to get aft and do her "duty" and still have time to reach her own seat.

During that time the concentration of the pilots was about to reach the big moment—sneaking out below the weather expecting the rainsoaked runway to be just ahead.

The landing gear was down; likewise the landing flaps; and the tower had cleared the plane to land. Out of the low hanging clouds and rain struggled the sturdy DC-3.

Only then did the cockpit door bang open and a highly excited flight attendant come rushing in shouting: "Go around, go around!"

At that point neither pilot had time to waste; they either landed right then, or increased power to maximum, and climb back into the soupy weather. Circling the field below the clouds was impossible.

The captain instinctively chose the logical course of action—nose up and climb for altitude. Having a discussion about the matter or giving it further thought was out of the question. He simply started giving the ground below a lot of distance.

That part of the flight suddenly became what is called a "missed approach," and once started, there is fast action in the cockpit. When the plane is back in the clouds and there are less opportunities for confusion, the captain starts to find out "how come the demand for a go-around?"

Naturally in this case he called the stew forward to find out why she felt the go-around was necessary.

"Well because," she told him, "I never got the signal to put the tailwheel down!"

So far as is known, that captain never got rid of the egg on his face or tried that trick again.

Because FAA regulations required only one flight attendant for all the seats you could safely jam into the old DC-3, airline management saw no need to add an additional stewardess. As a result, the one young lady ran the cabin. Unless the plane was still on the ground and she needed help, her chances for getting help were pretty close to zero. Occasionally there was a real touchy bit of action during flight, such as an unruly passenger, then one of the pilots would walk back and give the poor gal some assistance. However, in most cases the flight attendant would handle the problem, and do it well.

After bouncing around in the cabin caring for a seemingly limitless number of passengers—some nervous, grouchy or both—most stewardesses were simply eager to sit and rest. But there was an occasional flight attendant who learned how to do all that hard work smilingly and yet when playtime came, she joined in with enthusiasm.

That was the case of a young lady whose long day ended in what was considered a "one-horse" town. The crew and plane would layover until early next morning when it was scheduled to head back to home base.

The crew had rooms assigned at a small hotel about twenty minutes from the airport. Once reaching the hotel, the two pilots had dinner together and were ready for bed by 9:30.

Not so our hard-working cabin attendant.

A party-minded group of station agents had made it a point to invite our like-minded flight attendant to join them, and she did.

It must have been an active event, because at two a.m. the hard-charging stew returned to the hotel and banged on the pilots' door. She was already quite well saturated with the juice of the grape, but had no intention of letting that start go to waste. She wanted the pilots up—keep the party going.

There was no chance the pilots were going to play that game. Each remembered they were due to leap out of bed at 4 a.m. just to start up the next day's work schedule.

They did their best to coax the girl into her room for even a little bit of shut-eye, but she would have none of it.

Finally both pilots could tell she wasn't about to worry over any lost sleep, and they told her to "get to bed or we're going to give you a cold shower!"

That message didn't quite reach her. She still wanted to party.
The pilots both agreed they had no choice. They needed this little lady to be aboard that airplane at six in the morning.

They simply picked her up, carried her to her room, took off all her clothes, and shoved her smack into a cold shower!

The captain volunteered later he had never heard such language even from a mule-skinner! But they got her to bed and she stayed there.

Up at four, the pilots could hardly wait to learn what kind of a problem they faced. At the very least they expected they would have to wake her.

The hard-partying girl was not only up, she was dressed and ready to go.

The captain said her hair was still wet and her eyes had a tinge of red, but no one would have guessed what kind of a night she'd had.

"Surprised, too," said the captain, "she never said a bloody word about the two of us having popped her into the shower."

Whether she didn't remember or chose to say nothing about it, no one ever knew.

Back in 1966 a West Coast Airlines' DC-3 flight was about ready to cross the radio navigation fix at Wenatchee, Washington. right on its assigned course at eight thousand feet, when the stew decided she had time to visit the cockpit.

She hadn't been up front for more than a few seconds when this small white light on the pilots' instrument panel began a persistent blinking. Of course, both pilots knew that light only came on when the plane was passing over what is called a VOR—a high-frequency radio navigational station. A simple device to confirm to the pilots their instruments were doing a good job.

It quickly became obvious the girl had never seen the light before, because her very first comment was: "What's the white light for?"

Quick as a wink, the sharp-witted young captain answered:

"Why that tells us a virgin just entered the cockpit."

Then, in a reply just as quick, and in a voice that didn't hide the insult she'd felt:

"Wellll, you'd better get that damned thing fixed!!"

It must be obvious by now a few young ladies might have gotten their noses out of joint because one or more pilots took advantage of the girls' innocence. That may well have been the start of concern over sexual harassment.

For example, one new girl came aboard her scheduled aircraft for the day, met her captain and after a few questions from him, learned her brief indoctrination and training had been incomplete. She hadn't been taught about a very important item— flushing of the DC-3's toilet.

The captain said he "was truly surprised to find out" about this oversight, and he explained some "extra aspects" of her duties. As both of them moved toward the cockpit:

"You know," he said, straight faced, "each time one of your passengers has used the lavatory, for the sake of the other folks, it's up to you to see that the toilet gets flushed."

And, continued the captain, "the positive control for that is located here in the cockpit. You can't miss it. See? It's right along side of the copilot's seat. Just be sure each time you have to use it, you pump it real hard at least ten times."

"Right," she nodded, "I've got it."

As the day wore on she'd come bursting into the cockpit door two or three times each flight and pump that DC-3's lever faster than any copilot had ever been known to, then she'd rush back to continue catering to her passengers.

The poor girl really worked at it and of course her devilish tormentors spent a good part of the day laughing at the young stew's gullible nature.

Of course the toilet didn't receive any special benefit from her continued efforts.

All she'd done each time was pump up the aircraft hydraulic system a few pounds.

Then there's that chap from "Down Under".. an Aussie who grew up in airplanes and eventually ended up a chief pilot for his airline in "Ah'strylya."

The way a captain named Peter told this story on himself, he and this DC-3 were flying over a long stretch of wide open country... probably en route to Alice Springs out in the middle of nowhere.

Maybe there was a dozen passengers plus or minus, and of course the stew and a copilot.

The stew had only been on the job a short time. Apparently one of the passengers asked her to find out what specific spot the DC-3 was flying over on their route to wherever.

"She came up front and passed that question to us," said Peter, "and we told her: `Why don't you come back in a little while. We'll have the information for you then.'"

Some time passed and the passenger again asked her to inquire as to what their present position might be.

When she popped her head into the cockpit the second time asking the original question, Peter gave her this answer:

"Well, at this point we're not really certain, but we are making good time and we have lots of petrol...why don't you check with us a little later?"

After another 15 or 20 minutes she came back for the latest answer and got the frank admission the pilots were just not sure, but intended to find out shortly.

Peter told her: "Not too important, really. We have parachutes if we need to use them... we can just bloody well bail out."

The stew went a little white and sputtered: "But what about the passengers? They don't have any parachutes."

"Oh bother with the passengers," replied Peter, "we can always get passengers. What one can't always find are enough pilots."

The surprised stew went back to her cabin shaken, but it was time to prepare and serve the in-flight lunch, in which the pilots would share. As she was finishing preparation of the food she spoke to the pilots on the interphone and said she'd be up in a moment with the meals.

After the pilots got that message they hurriedly put the plane on automatic pilot; opened the cockpit side windows, (known to be used as emergency exits) got out of their seats and hid in the forward baggage compartment.

When the stew entered the cockpit with two trays of food, and discovered there was no one in the cockpit, it blew her mind! Looking at those empty cockpit seats and recalling the captain's earlier mention of parachutes, the startled girl dropped both trays; let out a blood curdling scream and turned to run for the passenger cabin.

As she did so, the pilots suddenly realized the little joke had suddenly blown up in their faces. As the terrified girl dashed back toward the passengers, the copilot managed to stick one arm out and grab the panicked stew when she ran by. So forceful was the girl's exit, she was not stopped, her momentum only slowed.

She fell halfway through the cockpit door with the pilot's hands all over her and both crewmembers on the floor in full view of all the passengers.

That little gag proved to be a costly one. Both pilots were grounded for a month.

The next tale isn't exactly sexual harassment, but it could well be called abuse. Remember the old four-engine DC-6 propeller aircraft?.. when it took eight hours or more to make a coast-to-coast flight?

Each of those planes in passenger service always had a minimum of two flight attendants. The senior one in the group ran the cabin, and as a rule it was that person's job to do all of the official business with the captain.

On board this one particular DC-6 trip was a crusty old captain who had been around the airline for 30 years. He looked at his job in a professional way and he expected his fellow crew members to feel the same about theirs.

His flight was already a little late because of the large number of other airliners that had been cleared from the Los Angeles terminal before him. The taxiway to the duty runway was filled with aircraft. And it was no joy for the captain to realize his departure was going to be further delayed because eight to ten other planes were lined up ahead of him.

To be frank, it turned him into a growler. He was mad. It's easy to see how a fellow in his position could get irritable over a new issue that popped up. Any issue!

An extra pilot, a non-official member of the crew (commonly called a 'deadhead') was riding up in the cockpit. He filled what everyone in the business referred to as the 'jumpseat.' In the DC-6 that seat was located right next to the door leading back to the cabin. Anyone trying to leave or enter the cockpit had to pass right by that jumpseat.

Sometime after the plane had departed the terminal building, the senior stewardess opens the cockpit door and squeezes by the deadheading pilot. She had come forward to do just what she was obligated to do—tell the captain the passengers were all strapped in and the cabin was set for takeoff.

After she had entered the cockpit, she could have waited long enough for the captain to stop talking before she passed her message, and she could have said:

"Captain sir, the cabin is set for takeoff."

But she didn't.

It was also unfortunate the poor dear had no idea the captain had let his irritation reach the boiling point.

She came through the door with enthusiasm and shouts to him:

"O.K. kiddo, we're all set back here."

Oooo...that did it!

Right there on the taxiway the salty old captain requested the little lady's undivided attention. She was too flip for him and he proceeded to chew her up one side and down the other. Must have gone on for ten minutes!

The way the deadhead pilot reported this tale, everybody else in the cockpit felt sorry for the poor girl, but he was the only one who could dare do something sympathetic to ease the pain. When the stewardess turned in quiet anger to depart for the passenger cabin, the deadhead simply reached over to open the door for her.

She shook him off.

"Don't bother," she said rather sarcastically, "I can crawl under."

An English training aircraft first created in the 1920's by the DeHavilland Aircraft Co. The plane shown here is the DH-82 "Tiger Moth," a 1930's development of a long series Brit pilots simply call "Moths." Hardly a pilot exists in the United Kingdom who has never flown a DeHavilland "Moth" of one model or another. For decades it was the standard basic trainer for the RAF.

Of recent vintage in combative aircraft, this airborne British "Tornado" is pictured getting refueled in what has become the current fashion: "Petrol okay, but we don't check tires or wash windshields." Inflight refueling has become commonplace for all major military aircraft except, of course, the tankers themselves.

What relaxed flying was all about
The Piper Cub

While numerous aircraft companies built what was called the "private plane" during the 1930s and 40s, only the Piper Cub (model J-3 here) seems to have been a remembered name to John Q. Public. People all over the nation frequently call any small, light aircraft a "Piper Cub," and it was a truly fine aircraft. Many are still restored and sought after to this day.

TO EACH HIS OWN

Living in the era of "political correctness," one might find it easy to classify the following story of yesteryear as being offensive or even subtle sexual harassment. But for two young airline pilots at the time, it was simply an example of virile males being alert, observing and appreciative.

Viva le femme!

The two DC-3 pilots involved were heading for the aircraft flight line to ready their airliner for the first trip of the day. The daily flight schedule in the dispatch office had shown they were to be accompanied on their day's flights by a stewardess whose name was totally unfamiliar. When the pilots arrived at their aircraft, the new "stew" had not yet arrived.

Busy at their own cockpit duties when the young lady did come aboard, they had yet to see her. Since the passengers were in the process of boarding and baggage had all been loaded, it was obvious to the pilots the novice stew was by now in the cabin and busy.

The pilots were nearly ready to accept the aircraft paperwork called the "weight & balance" report. Each flight must have one before departure. Standard practice with many airlines at the time, was having that specific paperwork be clipped to the end of a long, slim pole. The station agent at each stop would push such a pole up to the open cockpit window where the pilot could reach it.

But that didn't happen on this first leg of the DC-3's journey. The agent with the paperwork was helping the stewardess close up the passenger cabin's door and took advantage of her presence to hand her the report, requesting she deliver same to the pilots.

As it turned out, the stewardess was on her very first trip; determined to prove her willingness to help in any way she could. She accepted the weight & balance report without question, undoubtedly assuming her delivery of it was customary.

Up she went to the cockpit, paperwork in hand, arriving just as the two pilots were completing their check of the cockpit and its equipment. She stood there a second or two and finally said:

"What'll I do with this piece of paper?"

Both pilots turned around at the same time and.. *Voila!*..got their first look at the rest of their crew. They were duly impressed. (As if *she* may have had a.. uh.. "weight & balance" problem!) She was a most attractive addition to the trip.

For a brief moment, both pilots were speechless. The captain a bit slow on the draw; the young copilot quickly absorbing her outstanding attributes and the fact she was dressed in a rather loose fitting blouse. *Oo-la-la!*

The copilot sensing future possibilities quickly renewed his ability to communicate. He suggested she reach forward and drop the paperwork in the cockpit crew's catch-all spot.

To set the scene completely, a DC-3 cockpit is none too large. The two seats—one on each side—bracket the central, 30-inch-high control pedestal. Our cute young lady is standing as far forward as she can get, right behind said pedestal, slightly to the rear of each of the pilot seats. Towards the rear of the pedestal are located throttle handles, controls for propellers and good stuff like that. But forward of those temporarily unimportant things is a flat place that became the catch-all spot.

Now from where our cockpit visitor was standing, that catch-all spot was quite a little stretch. But of course the alert young copilot anticipated her having to stretch and bend when she placed the report on that empty space.

She promptly did exactly what the copilot intended while both of those intrigued pilots sat there looking over her shoulders, fairly captivated by the two-second display.

Coup de maitre!

For the rest of the day the pilots radioed each of the various station agents:

"Be sure and hand that weight and balance form to the stew. Don't put it on the 'stick.'"

At each stop she was a good stewardess, and certain she was carrying something(?) up forward the pilots would be anxious to see.

Obviously the Chief Stewardess eventually got wind of the new girl's unconscious but appreciated effort. Just as obviously the Chief Stew understood the "paperwork" wasn't why the pilots had been interested. Only a day elapsed before the 'revised' program of weight & balance delivery went back to the standard—and less inviting—procedure.

Of course, there is no *real* assurance fantasies can't come true, is there?

And eventually all of us air travelers either utilize or fantasize about using the airline's "first class" service. Even though most of us work-a-day people may never enjoy the real thing, it always sounds like the most glamorous way to go. Big, wide, cushiony seats.. all with enough leg room for a professional basketball player.. lotsa free drinks.. cuisine that often rivals Maxim's. All those features plus flight attendants who cater to your every need.

But.. tickets for first class seats usually cost big bucks, and "frequent flier" benefits aren't all they're cracked up to be. Just don't give up; keep trying.

However.. this short tale of a first class experience was rather a one-time deal. Two girl friends on a trip; "coach" tickets; no frequent flier awards involved.

But they sure picked the right airline and the right time to visit Greece!

It was 1971. Their chosen airline out of New York for Paris and on to Athens was Olympic. The flight was what many travelers call the "red eye." Whether sleep comes, you have to make the best of it, because the trip takes off in the late evening and flies all through the night.

Our two young ladies—one lived in Texas, the other in Hawaii—were longtime friends but hadn't seen each other for well over a year. Their rendezvous occurred in New York City. Their lives had been a long spell of no personal, verbal contact. Naturally the girls had a lot of catching-up to do.

Right from takeoff they were noticeably busy making up for all that lost time. Maybe they hardly noticed, but their assigned coach seats were up in the very first row; with everything forward of them blocked off by a massive set of curtains.

Anyhow, their talking continued unabated for an indefinite time after departure until a flight steward from the forward section approached. He quietly asked if they wouldn't like to enjoy sitting "up front."

Neither of them had to be super-smart to know that "up front" meant the first class section. Each of the thrilled young ladies immediately echoed the same response: "Yes," not really bothering to notice they had been the only recipients of the offer. Hey!.. how good can it get?

As they joyfully passed through the curtains to the more forward part of the cabin, it was clearly obvious there were curtained "compartments" on either side of the aisle. Even farther ahead was a partition through which they passed.

Before them was the most beautiful lounge either had ever seen on an airliner. There was virtually nothing that resembled an aircraft cabin. A big round table was nearly surrounded by booth-type seats.. the table "properly" equipped with a large bowl of fruit and a bottle of chilled champagne. Neither of the girls could understand why no one else was occupying such sumptuous accommodations.

Their comment: "It was *heavenly!* We were treated like royalty.. we talked the whole trip."

The gods of aerial endeavors had been most favorable.

Eventually they learned who had deemed them worthy of such fantastic surroundings. A gentleman approached who wore nothing resembling an airline uniform. He identified himself as a bodyguard. It quickly became evident the gods of flight had not been involved. It had been a special offer.. request.. whatever, of the airline's owner.

"You mean.. Mr. "O," himself??"

"Correct," said the bodyguard, "Mr. Onassis.. Ari Onassis."

"Wow.. no kidding?"

"No keeding," volunteered the bodyguard. "Mr. Onassis was trying to sleep in his compartment just forward of your coach seats. Your talking had been disturbing him. When he awakes you will be returned to your original seats."

Sure enough.. thirty minutes before the landing at Athens, Mr. "O" himself is up and thanked the ladies for their cooperation.

Probably safe to say the ladies did not receive the benefits of such an opulent setting on their return trip.

And speaking of opulent settings, back in the late '40's you shoulda seen the digs of Terry the bachelor officer. Terrence was a lieutenant at a U. S. Navy base in Morocco, NW Africa. He had been flying out of the Port Lyautey airfield there for nearly two years. It was kind of like home.

When Terry is a long-term resident—no matter where he is—he tends to redecorate and/or modify his digs to suit himself. (Take it from a friend.. he *does* make changes.) This "pad" of his was one of the more choice set of quarters at the base's BOQ... (bachelor officers' quarters)... even before Terry's elegant, added touch.

Terry, whose duty as a pilot caused him to travel a great deal in air transport planes throughout the Mediterranean and up into Europe. Naturally, over the course of many months, this self-styled interior decorator had often come off trips with any number of paintings, posters.. mid-eastern rugs.. probably some unique World War II souvenirs, as well. The walls and floors of his quarters were covered with a variety of items.

The day arrived when Terry was greeted by a surprise announcement. He would have to move to lesser quarters.

"Why?" quizzed the irritated Terry, "I like it. I've been there for nearly two years.. why the hell do I have to move?"

"Well," explained the BOQ bossman, "we have an officer just checked in who wants that room.. he's going to be here for three months and he outranks you by a year or so. You'll have to move."

"I'll be a s.." exploded Terry, "You mean a rookie lieutenant commander—a transit, at that—is going to boot me out of *my* room?"

"Yep, that's it," said the BOQ manager, "and I don't think he wants to wait too long."

Now Terry may have been burning over the deal, but he rarely loses his cool.. his brain is always ready to foil the opposition. He whips into the project with great zest. Everything he owns is stacked out in the hallway, then he trots off to the base paint locker.

Terry comes back with paint, brushes and all the stuff he thinks he needs. Right away, he's whipping through the place.. walls, ceiling, window frames.. everything. All newly painted.

Black! Solid, unadulterated black.

If he was going to be a decorator he obviously had to back off and take a long look at the results of his effort. Terry felt there just wasn't enough life to his work.. something was missing.

Back to the base paint locker. He acquired another gallon of trim; a smaller, more delicate brush. And back to work.

His masterpiece completed. He looked at it with admiration. "That'll keep the SOB awake."

Now the walls and ceiling looked back at Terry.

Eyes.. hundreds of eyes. All of them yellow.

No sooner had he crammed all of his belongings into new and lesser quarters, Terry goes out flying. He was airing out (pun intended) his gripes. When he returned, there was a message for him:

"Please see the Executive Officer."

So Terry buzzes off in his jeep to find the XO practicing a few short iron shots. "You wanna see me, Commander?"

"Yes, I do," says the second-in-command, "What's this stuff about you painting your room?"

"Well sir," replies the straight-faced Terry, "I've been living in it for two years... never been repainted all the time I've been in it. I thought it was the thing to do."

The XO didn't exactly cotton to Terry's decision, but as long as Terry was so interested in that kind of work, the XO ordered him to repaint the place. "And use some better judgement this time."

Terry decided a gray might be nice.. battleship gray. The Navy always had plenty of battleship gray.

And Terry got plenty. Several gallons. He must have put four coats of heavy gray paint over every inch of the place. Enough so it wouldn't become totally dry for 3 months! The odor of that oil-based paint would last for weeks!

Terry always had the feeling the officer who had forced him out of his choice quarters never really got a chance to enjoy the place.

However, Terry wasn't there to find out.

Within a day or so after his second attempt at redecorating, there was another message for him. It was from the base commander:

"Please see me. At once."

Terry is not one to pass up an order from a Navy captain. He promptly made the requested appearance.

The captain had some rather personalized viewpoints about Terry's attitude in dealing with others, even though Terry hadn't violated any orders. The captain figured Terry wasn't too likely to play a major part in maintaining harmonious relations within the captain's command, so he said:

"I'm going to have you transferred back to London."

As a long-time acquaintance of the blue-eyed Irishman, the author knows full well Terry probably took that news with a flow of crocodile tears. And, his old room was certainly available.

There are many passengers who fly almost as much as the airline flight crews. People flock to Singapore, London, Rome.. all those far off and famous cities. And there are U. S. presidential wannabees every four years who fly to nearly every state in the union—some land in three or four of the nation's states in one day. Obviously flying is here to stay and can help gratify nearly every need.

And it is doubtful anyone could make a claim the democratic voting process had received any greater support from aviation than the incident that happened early in 1996.

You may have trouble believing what pains a man would take to exercise what all "free" peoples believe are their inherent rights and obligations—to vote.. for the president of their country.. to do their duty!

The man of whom we speak lived in New York, though he was not a citizen of the United States. He was a resident alien, but a person having a passionate belief in the power and meaning of the ballot.

That feeling was so intense, when his country went to the polls to elect a president in March 1996, our man was well on his aerial trek "home." The next day would be election day in his country. When the tiring flight from New York landed, it *was* the next day. He went to the polls; voted, and promptly hustled himself back to the international airport where he boarded a return flight to New York.

His trip of dedicated citizenship was not a short one. Indeed, it was exceptionally lengthy. It took him a weekend. Amazingly, he had flown to Taiwan, in the western Pacific. The distance of his round-trip flight: Nearly 24,000 miles!

How patriotic can you get?

Thinking of that gentleman traveling a distance almost equal to a trip around the globe leads us into another story.. not a great story, just a down-home friendly type.

Humor is least expected when inbound and outbound airport traffic is heavy. Often a slight undertone of irritation is evident in the radio calls from the numerous planes. Occasionally a clever and unusual bit of chatter offers a welcome and momentary release from whatever tension prevails.

Many, if not all pilots in the general approach control area are tuned in on a specific air traffic control frequency. It's understood by all parties who use aircraft radio that keeping communications short is the right thing to do. Idle or extended commentary is officially unappreciated. While the FAA doesn't exactly stand guard over what's said on the air, the FAA does press the point about how to communicate effectively.

But once in awhile air traffic controllers and pilots let themselves slip just a bit.

Like on a busy day several years ago when Captain Mike was flying inbound, less than 20 miles from his destination. Mike's DC9 had been transferred to Approach Control's frequency.

The Approach controller's job is directing traffic into the immediate vicinity of the airport. In doing so, planes may be required to take new altitudes or to change their headings.

The controller was directing Mike's and several other flights when an inbound newcomer to the traffic—World Airlines— announced its arrival.

Suddenly the controller called Mike's aircraft and asked: "Do you have World in sight?"

Mike assured the controller: "Roger, we do."

The controller directed Mike to: "turn left and fly around World."

Mike-the-joker's quick response: "Well... okay, but would you mind if we landed first to get some more fuel?"

All the off-beat comments heard on various air control frequencies aren't sweetness-and-light. As witness this one case within a large airport environment recently:

In crowded skies the air traffic controller is most often in a stressful position, hassled by a combination of events and aircraft needs. This tale deals with a female controller pressed for quick responses from a sky full of airplanes and pilots.

Our responsible lady apparently showed her irritation at pilots apparently unable or unwilling to abide by her commands. In giving traffic directions, her voice soon became noticeably more shrill and sharp.

One pilot on the frequency queried the controller with this brief message: "Approach Control, over?"

The harried lady came back quickly and sharply: "Aircraft calling Approach, identify yourself."

The pilot's response: "Are you my ex-wife?"

Maybe this little nip of aviation life isn't the kind of humor that would appeal to everyone.. but let's try it on you and see if you can visualize the picture. (You receive the educational material for free.)

One of the Douglas DC-9's had just loaded passengers and left the terminal for the takeoff runway. Taxiing out, the cockpit crew finished up the "taxi" check list which consists of numerous items the crew performs before every departure. Taxi time to the runway was short and their aircraft being first in line, the crew accepted the tower's clearance for takeoff, proceeding at the same time with the "takeoff" check list.

The takeoff check list includes, among other items, snapping the ON switch for the anti-skid braking system. The copilot calls out the appropriate action. The captain's obligation is to be certain the switch is ON which is supposed to activate an orange-colored light informing the crew the system is "armed" and ready for dependable service. In this instance, the captain's usual precise response came up different—to the equivalent of "No way, Jose."

The anti-skid system just refused to be armed.

When an unexpected happening such as that occurs, it puts a hold on the planned takeoff.

"Is the anti-skid circuit breaker in?" was the question. Neither of the pilots could guess why, but it wasn't. Nothing would do but call the tower; cancel the takeoff clearance; explain they "had a problem" and ask permission to pull off to the side of the wide taxiway to park.

Tower heard all that; canceled the takeoff, and granted permission to park "clear of the taxiway centerline to permit another jet (a competitor's) to pass."

Everything electrical in the DC-9—it seems—is protected by circuit breakers in a huge panel of buttons immediately behind the captain's seat. The anti-skid CB is right at the top of the panel, easily seen by the copilot, but not something he can reach from his side of the airplane, nor is it practical for the captain to reach it while seated in his normal position.

"I'll check that CB," volunteers the captain, "maybe we can get our anti-skid system back again."

After stopping the aircraft and setting the brakes, the captain turns all the way around and is facing the circuit breaker panel behind his seat just as the competitor goes taxiing by on the left. That aircraft being on the same radio frequency, and having heard the DC-9's mention of a problem, looks in on the parked aircraft's cockpit with its captain facing rearward and says, jokingly, over the radio:

"Hey.. we see your problem. The captain has his head on backwards."

Well, okay. How about this one? The tale of the ancient airline pilot who memorized virtually every word and graphic information

about his routine flights. He did so well, he carried his flight bag—
(i.e. brain bag)—as the regulations require, but most of the copilots
had never seen him open it.

That captain was flying all month with the same copilot, a guy
who took offense at occasionally being asked by the captain to look
up unusual stuff. The copilot had been asked to open his *own* bag to
find what the captain wanted. (Both pilots knew, of course, that every
brain bag in the airline contained identical material, all information
required by the regulations.)

"So why doesn't that lazy SOB ever open up *his* bag?" the copilot
said to himself. Well, there was no way any copilot could really argue
with a captain when that copilot is directed to do something as simple
as dig out some material the captain wanted. But the whole situation
began to bug him. Finally he came up with an idea that would at least
make the ol' geezer have to work a little harder.

Between flights, most pilots placed their brain bags in the dispatch
office where they'd be handy when needed. The copilot knew that,
because he left his there, as well.

Next day the copilot, carrying an every day brick, eased into
dispatch before the captain was likely to be on the scene. He carefully
opened the captain's bag, and shoved the brick underneath all of the
manuals.

When it came time for the flight, naturally the captain picked up
his bag and carried it, as always, to his assigned aircraft, but he made
no comment.

Second day, this whole procedure was repeated, but of course by
that time there was the surreptitious placing of the *second* brick. The
captain began to notice the strain it had become to carry "that damned
bag." But perhaps he didn't let on to his copilot, for that copilot added
another brick to the bag.

That must have been too much for the ol' captain. He cancelled
out his flights after the "third brick" day and checked in with his
doctor. By all reports, the medic suggested he get another examination
and perhaps take four or five days of sick leave. In any case, the
captain wasn't around for a like number of days.

When the copilot heard about the captain actually being on sick
leave, (there was even a rumor he was in the hospital) that got the
copilot worried. "Maybe I've gone too far," he confided to one of his
buddies. He immediately went over to the dispatch office; found his
captain's bag, and removed all three of the bricks.

On the captain's first day back to work, the guilty copilot felt so badly about the trick he played, he deliberately avoided the captain in dispatch and walked out early to their assigned aircraft.

Eventually, the copilot had to face him, so when the captain arrived in the cockpit, the copilot greeted him: "Good morning, Captain," he said rather nervously, "Glad to see you back. Heard you were under the weather. Sure hope you're okay," said the concerned copilot.

"Well I don't know what caused my problem," said the captain, "but I sure feel much stronger now."

In times of stress and disorder, the injection of humor into serious situations definitely has its place. What's more, it's been known to work. Keeping a "cool head" is important, for any element of panic among people invariably creates more of the same. Quite obviously, there is no room for panic in the close confines of an aircraft.

One of the author's friends who truly believes in the theory is a retired military man. He's was an Army Ranger in the Korean conflict more than 40 years ago. Now he occasionally uses the benefits he earned by occasionally taking a flight to "somewhere" (on a space available basis) in Air Force transport planes. He has the time; has no worries about a spouse, and he knows the price is right.

On one occasion of transpacific flying, Bill, we call him, had managed to find a huge C-141 "Starlifter" transport that was going his way.

Like the commercial airlines, flight crews of Military Airlift aircraft work hard to be certain all of their passengers get "the word" on the safety procedures aboard the various airplanes in which they are flying. A briefing on the life saving equipment is presented "just in case there is an emergency." For travel in high-flying jets, that safety message, no different from any airline, always includes the details on how to use the oxygen masks. When Bill boarded as the only guy dressed in "civvies," (the other 60 or so were active duty military people) he never anticipated having to see those oxygen masks fall.

Somewhere in the flight, however, that 'stress and disorder' problem was suddenly and noticeably present. The aircraft was at high altitude—about 35,000 feet—when there was a loss of cabin pressure; the oxygen masks dropped, and the aircraft began a hurried descent to lower elevations!

That awesome feeling of being in real trouble enveloped some of the young military men surrounding Bill. They were having second thoughts about their immediate future.

Bill took their reaction as one deserving of a brief, but poignant note of humor.

As he reached for the mask, he commented to the young man seated next to him:

"Oh well, the last plane I was on, I parachuted out of."

(Ed. note: He did. A month earlier he made a jump purely for recreation.)

And Bill thought his comment was an example of good spontaneous, possibly pacifying humor.

Not so, his young seat-mate! The kid not only failed to voice a chuckle, his eyes were shiny glass balls shimmering with fear.. and from a rather constricted throat, the exclamation:

"But..but.. *We ain't got no parachutes!*

Lockheed "done good!"
Some of the best aircraft ever built

The Lockheed-built P-38 "Lightning" served the USAAF in all theaters of combat, ringing up a fabulous score of "kills." Early in 1990, an unrestored P-38 found in Britain, was flown to Arizona across the North Atlantic via Iceland & Greenland by a daring Englishman.

The notorious Lockheed "U-2," a super-secret reconnaissance aircraft specifically designed to fly higher and farther than any other single-engine jet plane in the world. It needed to, for it was initially used to overfly countries with whom the United States was involved in what was called the Cold War, an era that lasted until 1989. It took a ground-to-air missile to bring one down in the Soviet Union in May 1960.

The P2V "Neptune" in silhouette at midnight against the Alaskan summer sun near Point Barrow. The U.S. Navy's first such model made a record-setting non-stop, unrefueled flight from Perth, Australia, to Columbus, Ohio, USA, in 1946.

TO GHANA WITH LOVE

Aviation obviously flourishes everywhere. Even in the countries of the so-called "Third World." In west Africa, for example, one country has been using its airline as a means of heightening the nation's image for twenty years.

At the outset, airports within their area of operations existed but few had any of the niceties found in their counterparts throughout the western world. Dependability of service bore little resemblance to operations in the U. S.

Never mind the fact the country's phones barely worked; that roads were little more than trails; that entire families left their bushland mud huts to make new homes out of the cities' industrial trash. In the seventies, leaders of Ghana saw the importance of using aviation to bridge the cultural gap between west Africa and the western world. They eagerly sought ways to accomplish it. How they and the supporting staff of services responded in 1976 is a story in itself.

Though its airline had initiated air service earlier in the decade, serving its near neighbors with jet planes was considered an added element of prestige.

Ghana chose the standard McDonnell-Douglas DC-9, a twin-engine jet passenger aircraft carrying 80-139 people and used extensively around the world over relatively short distances. Ghana ordered the desired number of aircraft from the California factory. Delivery dates, however, were far off in the future.

But Ghana couldn't wait to display its aviation prowess to its neighbors along the west African bulge. They called halfway around the world for assistance. The relatively small Hawaiian Airlines company agreed to provide what is termed a "wet lease"—meaning the aircraft plus flight and maintenance personnel for a contractual amount of money. Ghana Airlines would also use the American crews in the training of Ghanians.

Within the U.S. airline there were several applicants for the assignment—all from pilots and mechanics who had never experienced the sights, sounds and humidity of west Africa. At the outset the total list of six willing aviators plus five maintenance crew members made up the team.

Ghanian pilots were due to receive initial training from the McDonnell-Douglas Company in California. They were to return to Ghana after three-months, ready to fly as copilots to the three U.S. captains who were expected to support the operation for a one year stay.

For the American contract crew the whole affair was to be the experience of a lifetime. Financially, they would make more money than they made at home. But they were to re-learn a truism: Money isn't everything!

The project would be a learning process for more than just the Ghanians.

A 139-seat model DC-9 left the U.S. in October 1976 on a flight halfway around the globe. The final destination: Accra, Ghana. The trip to equatorial Africa went without a hitch.

Upon arrival the Americans were initially housed in a hotel until their promised houses were readied. From the very start, the ability to find food inviting to a typical Yankee was a challenge.. even in most restaurants. One pilot had the good sense to anticipate a scarcity of American type food. He arrived with a gigantic jar of peanut butter.

"His room and his personage," reports one of the pilots, "suddenly became extremely popular."

As per the contract, each of the pilots and mechanics not only was to be supplied with a house, but a car together with an abundant number of variously qualified servants. When the homes were staffed and ready, (most houses had been previously occupied by United Nations and embassy personnel) the Americans were duly invited to assume occupancy.

Totally awed by the huge size of most of the homes, each of the Americans could envision a lonely life if they each lived separately. They chose three of the houses and returned the remainder. And while the promised cars were there, the network of usable roads was noticeably minimal.

The surrounding environment caused the newcomers to openly suffer from a heavy dose of cultural shock. The presence of poverty at its lowest scale mixed upon occasion with ostentatious opulence provided a display of customs and traditions virtually unknown to the arriving Americans. Levels of sanitation and a number of usual amenities, not to mention quality and availability of foodstuffs, served to remind the incoming crews they were no longer in familiar territory.

The above factors, together with the hot, sticky weather at 300 miles above the equator, were sufficient to lessen their enthusiasm.

The initial impression: Ghana was a far piece from home.

"Frankly," said one pilot, "for our first week on the scene we had neither the courage nor the knowledge to eat out. Even the simple act of quaffing a glass of beer on the hotel's veranda was a contest—one between you and the flies. To us, a fly in one's beer called for a new glass; new beer. That brought out a laugh from a person with more local experience when he quickly realized I was a newcomer."

"We've got a joke about that," volunteered a British expatriate. "Your first year here, one asks for a new beer. During your second year, you simply dump the bloody fly out. In the third year, you just order a `fly.'"

"When we moved into our houses," said pilot Ralph Godbe, "shopping for food suddenly became a project. The only familiar items we found in one market were rice and Ghanian beer. Each shelf had a few boxes of Uncle Ben's rice. Beer and rice. Nothing else. Reportedly, the stock at any of the other markets was the same."

"We were used to rice, but every meal? Okay, we'll take the rice. Maybe we can have beer every meal, too."

"Beeah, yeh?" said the store manager, "whar arh yoah bottles, suh?"

"Bottles?" asked the pilots. "We don't have any bottles. We just arrived. We need bottles?"

"I am soree suh.. you have no bottles, you cahnot buy beeah. You bring da bottles, we sell you beeah." The new arrivees offered $5 for a case of bottles. The answer was still: "No bottles, no beeah." The urgency of the problem led the Americans to seek out a source of bottles. A Britisher flying with Ghana Airlines finally satisfied a thirst by locating the required containers.

Food—where and how to find it—became an issue with each of the Yanks. Almost as important as the level of flight safety they were to encounter.

The DC-9 aircraft had an ingrained safety record second to none, but it quickly became obvious maintaining that record while utilizing west African airways' facilities would be a challenge. The level of flight services to which pilots from the western world were accustomed did not exist.

Weather reports at times were not simply hours old, but days old. Reports of airport hazards rarely existed or were hopelessly outdated. While control towers worldwide use the English language as their standard appropriate method of voice communication, the Americans' ability to recognize what was assumed to be English was an everyday ailment.

Overbooking of flights quickly became a point of interest to the American contract crew. It was obvious there were some unscrupulous ticket agents all too willing to accept "dash," or a little extra on the side to "guarantee" their customers received seats on their preferred flights.

There were always more tickets sold than the plane had seats. When the inevitable arguments ensued, there were often several ticket holders who were denied seats and were, as one pilot put it, "literally airlifted off the aircraft." He himself relieved one irritated, potential passenger of a brandished knife.

If boredom were likely, a day's operations or the occasional armed coup against a west African government always enlivened working hours.

Just weeks following commencement of the contract, an American captain and his first officer arrived as scheduled in a country a short distance east of Ghana. Their request to land resulted in a rather confusing reply from the airport tower:

"You are cleared to land, but do not land." Using the best American logic, the captain decided the tower personnel wanted better identification of the plane and expected the aircraft to fly by the tower first.

He was right. "You are now cleared to land," volunteered the voice in the tower.

Following the landing, the captain began taxiing the DC-9 into the terminal area. As he did so, copilot Ralph Germann saw what he described as a bush literally moving from its original position. This interesting phenomenon captured his attention. The closer the aircraft got to the parking ramp, more "bushes" moved. As the plane came to a stop, the "bushes" suddenly became armed, camouflaged soldiers, many of whom were now rushing rapidly toward the aircraft, their assault rifles at the ready!

The typical American flight crew, frightened as they could be at the greeting party, quickly and correctly assumed the plane's exit stairway should be lowered; that the soldiers weren't playing war games. (Even before soldiers boarded the aircraft the crew observed the terminal and the control tower featured some broken windows and damage obviously resulting from bullets and small artillery shells.)

At the moment an entrance into the aircraft was ready for use, several of the armed soldiers rushed aboard. One came into the cockpit pointing his weapon first at one pilot and then the other; his finger on the trigger and the rifle's safety turned off! A worrisome point to the plane's crew. The soldiers looked as scared as the flight crew!

Soon the terrifying situation was vented into simple nervousness. The senior military person aboard apparently went through every passenger's passport and let certain passengers deplane. The station manager or his representative was allowed to brief the flight crew concerning the reason for the original level of hostility. The pilots were told the remainder of the passengers and the plane were both cleared to fly to their next destination.

The DC-9's frightening greeting had coincided with the follow up to an attempted *coup d'tat;* an event that had lasted through most of the previous night. A large four-engine jet had landed without approval during the night and disgorged approximately two hundred armed men intent upon forcibly taking over the country. Only a few hours prior to the DC-9's arrival, the attacking group had been badly defeated; reboarded their waiting jet and took off.

When the local government force-in-charge met the friendly DC9, they weren't taking any chances that the aircraft wasn't ferrying in another group of rebels.

By training and custom, Ghana's "imported" flight crew recognized the purpose of having a flight schedule. And Ghana's transportation leaders accepted the fact every airline should have one. So a schedule had been posted, as if to say: "Okay, we have one," but the airline's actual use of the schedule was apparently used to learn how late each of the arriving and departing aircraft had been. The various station managers seemed to have an inherent "no worry" attitude when it came to abiding by schedules.

Soon, however, somebody in Ghana Air recognized the value of on-time service.

The U.S. captains were given the responsibility of making an earnest attempt to keep the system on schedule.

Very early in the life of the contract, immediate efforts to rectify the "fly any ol' time" condition often resulted in fractured egos; the temporary stranding of passengers, and downright threatening words among the various citizens along the route. Those who weren't at the airport on time simply got left and rank had no privileges. Once the word got out, the number of passengers flying Ghana Airways actually increased.

When the author's friend Dean joined the group he went through some trying times attempting to convince various station personnel to display a sense of timeliness and to recognize schedules as a necessary part of their day's work. The station managers finally accepted the theory as sound, but political expediency often erased the practicality of the concept.

On one of Dean's scheduled departures from Monrovia, Liberia, passengers had been boarded, cargo was loaded and Dean was on time and ready.

"Cahptun suh," comes the request from the station manager, "we must ahsk for a fifteen minute d'lay for the president of Liberiah and his pahty."

Dean knew in advance the president and his group were listed for the trip but he felt obligated to live up to the terms of his contract with Ghana Air. His response to the station chief: "I'm sorry. We can't delay. We're closing the door."

"Cahptun, we cannot leave without the President. You must wait."

"Sorry," radioed Dean, "we're leaving."

"Suh, I will be thrown in jail if you should leave without him. Furthuh, I am telephoning the a'ahpoht towah to deny you pa'mission to staht yoah engines."

Dean thought that just may keep him on the ground as Tower permission was indeed required before a plane could fire up its engines. But Dean also knew the International Congress of Aviation Organizations took a dim view of flight controllers who were charged with delaying flights. ICAO's power was not unknown, even in Liberia. Dean invoked it, threatening the tower with a report to ICAO if his request for takeoff was delayed.

The directness worked. The flight went out on time and Monrovia became one of the better on-time stations all during the remainder of Dean's tour in Africa.

And the president?

None of the Americans learned how he accepted his missed connection.

Boeing Aircraft, builder of the popular "Stratocruiser" air transport, developed this C-97 military version for the U. S. Air Force in the decade of the 1950's. The famed Boeing B-29 and B-50 bombers of the 1940's were engineering forerunners in the creation of this aircraft. *(Author's note: "AirHuman" editor Ron Jensen piloted a C-97 like this in the story on hurricane winds over Wake Is.)*

P.S.

With apologies to Ron. We lost something in the transition to a black & white photo. The painting, from which this photo was taken, is much more effective.

Flying bigtime in plywood and 2 x 4's

Millionaire entrepeneur/pilot Howard Hughes, owner of Hughes Tool & Die Company, and a developer of aircraft, flew his gigantic eight-engine wooden flying boat on its only flight, November 2, 1947. The distance: One mile over Los Angeles harbor. The Hughes project was initiated by the federal government upon America's entry into World War II. After four years, the aircraft was still not completed. Only one was ever built. Today the "Spruce Goose" is homeported in McMinnville, Oregon.

THE AIRLINE'S TALENT

Everyone of us has a close friend or relative who is basically the nervous type. Someone whom we see intently grasping the arm rests of the airliner's seat once their plane begins to move.. the "white-knuckle" kind of passenger.

And maybe you're aware of a trip he or she is planning, to be riding a huge jetliner or a smaller commuter plane. If you believe there is a chance you can provide that person with some kind of assurance, why don't you try letting that individual read this?

First of all, anyone on a commercial airliner is as safe as.. well.. as safe as they once were on their mother's lap. Maybe even safer.

In my 42 years as a pilot, and now 14 more as a passenger, we always made it.

Can you call it "luck?" Not hardly. Airline safety doesn't just happen. Traveling safely in today's realm of flight is the result of years of engineering research and costly development of human skills. Thorough and effective planning permits hundreds of thousands of passengers to fly each day, safely and surely. It's a program that demands not only talent, but solid judgement.

Probably the first thing everyone should keep in mind is, when they are riding with a scheduled airline, they are dealing with professionals. Flight crews are people who have made a career out of being conscientious; at becoming supremely qualified for the work they are doing. Any evidence to the contrary is indeed a rarity.

And this is not a one-time qualification. Federal air carrier inspectors and the airline's own "check pilots" all ride herd on the pilots at various times during the year. In essence, all the people in the cockpit and in the cabin have to prove themselves time and time again.

You know why the pilots who fly your airliner are looking out for the passenger?.. why they have a direct and selfish interest in their customer's safety? Think about it a moment. If they *do* happen to have an accident, *they* are going to be the first ones at the scene!

Obviously the pilots are not too keen on putting themselves in that position.

"About their basic qualifications?.." some anxious person will ask.

Besides needing several years of flight experience, whether a pilot learned in the military or in the civilian market, a captain needs 1,500 pilot hours just to meet the government's technical requirements. In most cases—especially your well known older airlines—they would sneer at 1,500 hours and say: "Just a beginner!" and there is no way that pilot would be captain of your aircraft. He or she might make a good copilot, but not a captain.

Over and above all that, just to be eligible to fly your airliner— even as a copilot—your flight deck crew spent twenty 8hour days in a government approved ground training class studying the mechanics and details of each model aircraft in which they will be flying. (Just because a pilot is qualified in one brand of airplane doesn't cut it if he or she is asked to fly in another type.) Each year pilots are required to take another week-long recurrent class as well as flight checks twice a year for each of the different type aircraft they might be asked to fly.

Your pilot's ability to fly any given model and to verify the thoroughness of the ground training classes is proven through actual flight and through amazingly realistic flight simulators. After the many hours of training the captain receives certification not from another airline employee but as a result of a long oral exam conducted by a Federal Aviation Administration inspector. The training program is then topped off by a flight test under the trained eye of an FAA pilot qualified in that model aircraft. (That same inspector may pop up any time during any of the captain's flights thereafter.)

Even after that, a check pilot who is more experienced in that model, rides as a "babysitter" in the cockpit with the new captain for as much as twenty-five hours.

Surprisingly—at least to me—enough of us feel quite secure when we ride in an auto, yet most of us are fully aware that tragedy on the highway is a daily event of gigantic proportions. Invariably those incidents are caused by one operator or another; seldom by mechanical failures.

See the difference between pilots of airplanes and drivers of cars?

Automobile drivers are seldom if ever called upon to really demonstrate their competence as the years go by. Pilots always are.

We're all proud of our modern automobiles, vehicles that are designed to negotiate endless miles of urban bedlam and frantic freeways. They're wonderful machines!

They just don't come equipped with the totally competent, trained driver.

That's where experienced airlines protect the passenger. It is the real key to their success. A better chauffeur you couldn't find.

Of course I'd be less than honest if I didn't admit to having had some doubts from time to time myself. There are times when flights failed to arrive when and where they were expected. Who can guarantee everything in life? Even the very best of professionals run afoul of problems once or twice in their lives, so no one can make any 100% assurances.

The relatively rare and tragic incidents that do occur are always spectacular enough to make today's news media hasten to put them on display. The fact such events *are* news is because they happen so seldom.

But still, the facts are: Transportation safety records will confirm your airliner flight is much safer than any trip you'll take in an auto.

Frankly, I suspect one of the reasons most of us accept the extremely heavy loss of life on our highways is because we have come to expect it.

Now take a quick look at your airliner. From the aspect of dependability, sturdiness, endurance and weight reduction your airliner is ten times more advanced than your car. Everyone in the aeronautical engineering and design business remembers that if something does go wrong while a plane is in the air, your pilot is not free to pull over and park.

So the airliner is designed, built, and maintained to fly in spite of equipment failures. Virtually every part in the aircraft has a duplicate aboard—sometimes more—each of which can enable the plane to continue flight and to land safely.

We call it system redundancy.

Be assured... Whoever put your airplane together really built it to last. For example: Your typical long-range jet coming into service today has engines designed to run almost forever, in any kind of weather. Just to be safe, however, after approximately eight million miles the engines are changed whether they need it or not.

If you're concerned about the condition of your car, you get someone to care for its parts to be sure they will all work. Chances are your car is checked over once every few months.

(That statement usually brings the comment: "Yeah.. but my car doesn't have to fly.")

True, and since an airliner obviously does, dozens of people go over every moving part as often as once a week. Experts in the fields of engines, electronics, hydraulics and airframes inspect or work on an airplane so often they know it like the back of their hand. Further, they are all licensed specifically for the work they've chosen.

For any specific journey, an hour before the flight the captain receives the information needed for that trip. Competent, trained persons across the nation—or even from major points around the globe—constantly update computers supplying route conditions, hazards, planned traffic deviations, temporary and permanent changes plus other useful information.

Then the captain and the dispatcher put their combined heads together for a last minute analysis. Their experience and expertise is utilized jointly for safety of flight for any trip. Each of them certify the flight plan they work up is the safest possible way for that airplane to make the flight. The Federal government demands they share that responsibility.

Their "togetherness act" means close attention has been given to the route of flight, weather, the winds en route, the condition of the navigational aids along the flight path, the limitations of the destination airport, terrain, fuel required, and other items. Within the space of an hour or two, several of those factors may suffer such changes that consideration is also given to alternate action.

In this business, nobody likes surprises.

Like so many endeavors in this complex world, a flight is a team effort. After the captain feels confident that the trip can be flown safely he discusses appropriate portions of the situation with the rest of the flight deck crew as well as those in the cabin.

Each flight has its variations—even over a route members of the crew have flown before. Flight attendants, for example, must be alerted to any expected weather that could cause disruption to the serving of meals, or to the general passenger comfort and safety.

The known presence of a jet stream with its high velocity winds may delight someone who is anxious to get home early, but it also can be an air mass containing some "bumpy" air. No one enjoys that and it is likely the pilots will ask for route and altitude changes that will make the flight more pleasurable. But good planning usually prevents changes like that.

If such changes are made, the cockpit crew will be ready to make corrections. For example, their fuel usage chart.. if the flight altitude is lower than originally planned, a jet uses more fuel. There may be additional or different reporting points to consider; the direction of flight will establish corrections to the navigation system that most certainly will require a check and double-check.

It is the flight deck crew who have the greatest need for all of the above information, for their primary job is to provide safety. Where they go, how they get there, is frequently more difficult than the average passenger can appreciate.

Prior to engine start the copilot may tell the captain one of the special little gidgets on his side of the cockpit "doesn't give me a good reading."

"Check it again," says the captain. "If it doesn't perform before we get to the runway, we can't go without it. It's on the MEL as mandatory." (That's the Minimum Equipment List, specifying exactly what must work before a flight can be legal to depart. Every airliner is equipped with an MEL, most often this so-called "list" is a book two inches thick. The list varies from one type of aircraft to another. The MEL is decreed by the FAA whose rules all U.S. carriers are obligated to abide by. Literally hundreds of items are on this list; each of them individually important to maximum safety of flight.)

And there are so many factors that can reduce the level of safety. Some of them directly involve passengers and their cooperation. Which brings up another point: Any requested actions one hears from the flight attendants are not contrived reasons to keep people from enjoying their flight. They come from regulations based totally upon experience—the probabilities and possibilities recognized and mandated by Federal law.

After the aircraft is readied and the loading of fuel, food, passengers and cargo is complete, the airliner advises an air traffic controller and receives a clearance to taxi and eventually to takeoff. Once airborne, pilots rarely just choose the course they desire to fly. Instead they typically fly specific headings, routes and altitudes worked up in advance that may, for reasons of other traffic, be altered by Air Traffic Control.

ATC people are as well trained and experienced in their duties as the pilots are in theirs. The controller is a 'groundling,' the air traffic coordinator who uses radio and radar. He or she must not only monitor the progress of one airliner, but know the precise speed, position and altitude of every other plane in his or her sector of the sky.

The controller supplements the input from radio and radar by using the experience of the pilot, who is the person fine-tuning every maneuver of the plane. The controller makes adjustments to each plane's journey as air traffic situations dictate. Short of an emergency, your pilot is obligated to follow the controller's commands.

When the controller uses radar to cross check direction of flight, altitude, air-(or Mach) speed, and distance from any given facility, the pilot does the same thing through the cockpit instruments, very high frequency radio stations, and the always useful radar. Long distance and over-ocean flights make use of much of the above over variable, coded route structures, special altitudes, and the incomparable accuracy of space satellites or inertial navigational systems that will pinpoint the aircraft's position over thousands of miles of travel.

Safe navigation involves an appreciable amount of verbal communication with nameless people on the earth's surface— primarily to keep aircraft separated from each other. But periodic weather and wind reports, both at the earth's surface and at flight altitude, are radioed skyward to provide the pilot with updated information that will lead to the safest routes and flight levels.

Indeed the factors mentioned are only part of what the modern airliner and its crew utilize (by both need and Federal requirement) to get the passenger into his or her next jetway.

Safety in airline operations is not a chancy thing. It is the key element protecting each passenger's desire to arrive safely at the proper destination.

Now.. how do you accept the cabin crew—the flight attendants?

Do airline passengers take the duties of the F/A's seriously? Maybe.. maybe not.

Most airline passengers expect smiles, sweet talk and good service. They go for the comfort and fast transportation. And in this highly competitive world, if an airline wishes to keep its customers happy, much of that effort is placed in the hands of the flight attendants.

But the flight attendants are always in a paradoxical position.

"How's that again??"

Well, in reality, the flight attendants' most important function is safety. It's a subject most of us air travelers never seriously consider. While the normal life of the flight attendants' business is usually all sweetness and peanuts, the real reason for their presence is *safety—*

yours! So, when (God forbid) a real or suspected emergency pops up on your flight, you'll find the happy talk disappearing in quick bursts of coldly clear, solid instructions on what *must* be done. Obviously a characteristic contrary to the public relations-oriented talents those flight attendants usually display.

But, should such an event occur, the flight crew must have passenger cooperation. You, the passenger, become an active participant. And it is during those rare moments when flight attendants all become tough. Forget the sugary words, for they tell *you*, the passenger, *what*, *how* and *when* to do whatever is required. Not surprisingly, federal law obligates all passengers to abide by *any and all instructions* issued by flight attendants.

The wise, safety-minded passenger pays attention.

Most of us are glad the safety of air travel has become almost a "given," but that benign look at safety causes us to become apathetic toward its real importance.

When the standard cabin announcements are made, casually storing the information in the subconscious just won't 'cut it,' but deep thought on the subject might.

As the Hawaiians might say: "Hey.. try listen!"

In other words, passengers shouldn't ever go unprepared. They should avoid an attitude of: "We've always arrived without any problems, right?"

Sorry to say, a relatively large number of passengers (frequent fliers, especially) appear to 'tune-out' the announcements about safety because "we've heard it all before." Repetition may mean the mind has memorized the announcements, which is good—up to a point. But during an emergency, just knowing the words and not visualizing the action required could leave a passenger wishing he or she had. The smart thing is to always consider what one would do; what one *has* to do. Having passengers cement the picture clearly in their minds is very valuable advice..

Here's a phrase that might sum it up: "Where immoderate action is required, use more than moderate thought." After all, we're talking about a once-in-your-life kind of action.

If—just if—the next airliner in which you are a passenger has a fairly non-hazardous incident such as the sudden appearance of the plane's oxygen masks. What are you going to do with yours? Let panic lock up your brain?.. maybe shout for the nearest flight attendant asking: "Where do I turn this thing on?" as dozen of other passengers face the same dilemma? True, it is a simple procedure, but no maneuver is simple when inadequate knowledge and lack of confidence can complicate it.

And the life jackets.. five bucks will get you a tenner, 20% of the passengers won't get their jackets on correctly without someone else's help.

Airlines know customers obviously want two things—safety and good service. Frankly, if the airline is reputable, the company seeks the same result. But they always put safety first.

Still, as we said, a high level of customer satisfaction is very important—except for the "white-knuckle" passengers, who will gratefully settle for safety only.

Repeating an old saying: "safety is important to the flight crew because their own precious lives are on the line, too." Passengers should try giving them trust, respect and attention. After all, the mix of smiling public relations and a mandatory safety program are rather unlikely partners.. to the dedicated flight attendant, concern over his or her obligations has all the makings of a stress filled day. It is not the simple "how do you like your coffee?" endeavor it may appear to be. Each flight attendant has to be well endowed with competency in keeping people happy, yet knowledgeable enough on technical matters to understand the mechanics of trouble, and to respond appropriately.

Recall one of your own trips.. if things really didn't go smoothly, (but your safety never appeared in doubt,) did you threaten never to fly with that airline again? Well, we all face exasperating situations.. in a crowded world, life is hardly ever hassle free.

Ponder over it.. just for a moment or two.

Perhaps how you think about your flight attendants' position will make a difference in how you enjoy your flight. Be considerate of your flight attendants. Each of them possess knowledge that may save your life. And they'll love you for your thoughtfulness.

How sporty can you get?

A sporty, all metal Ryan STA was one of the classics of the mid-1930s. Initially powered by a 125hp Menasco engine, as WW II approached America's shores, the Army Air Corps training command bought a far less attractive model equipped with a five cylinder Kinner engine and called it the PT-22.

One of the most famous classic aircraft in the U. S. is the D-17 Staggerwing built by Beech Aircraft Corp. While the unusual positioning of the top wing further aft than the lower wing proved noteworthy and very successful for Walter Beech in the late 1930s, the concept never caught on with other producers in the decades to follow.

War was not a pleasantry...
But flying was seldom dull

The Lockheed-Vega PV-1, a Navy patrol bomber derived from a 1930's airliner called the Lodestar. In World War II the author flew this model in nearly all areas of the Atlantic & Pacific Oceans.

SKILL WILL OUT

It was a typical January day in Bethel, Alaska: damp and plain cold! Residents with a deep desire to travel knew going by air was their only practical choice.

There were two people who not only had the desire, but the obligation—an Indian Health Service doctor normally based in Anchorage, 370 miles due east, and Maureen, the Bethel-based nutritionist fresh out of Hawaii. Both Maureen and the veteran physician servicing the broad delta of the Yukon-Kuskokwim rivers area had an appointment with more than 200 children in St. Mary's, 100 miles to the northwest. (Many of those scheduled to be seen that day had been delivered by this same doctor.)

The twosome had been ticketed to leave Bethel on the morning plane. When the two arrived at the Bethel airport, it was fogged in. The bad news was: "All flights were canceled for the remainder of the morning."

The duty-bound physician was not deterred by the uncooperative weather. He had "his kids to see" and old friendships to renew. "Let's go to the river," he suggested, "Someone should be flying."

Maureen had no grounds for doubting his expectations about finding a bush pilot or two, for the frozen Kuskokwim River in winter was a highway and an airport all in one; the ice thickening to as much as six feet.

Surprisingly the fog had not settled over the river and two small Cessna airplanes were being activated for flight. The good news was: the charter operator was hauling some cargo for St. Mary's and he would have two seats available.

The bad news was: The flight would cost twice what the scheduled airline charged.

"We stood on the wharf, shivering in the cold, anxiously watching the bush pilots and their helpers load each of the two planes," said Maureen. "When the first plane was loaded with its cargo, only one seat in the rear was available for a passenger and already the weight in the aircraft had definitely caused the tail to settle toward the ice runway."

To Maureen, the whole operation looked like a worrisome deal, and she shot a nervous look at the doctor. "But," she recalled, "he was too busy talking with our assigned pilot, a man who looked to be no more than twenty." She was nearly convinced "the pilot might well have been another of the `children' the doctor had delivered." It did not give Maureen confidence. In her short term experience with bush pilots, she had the impression "they were supposed to be more mature looking."

When Maureen next looked at the heavily laden, "tail low" aircraft, she saw the ground crew up on the wing chipping away at a collection of ice. (For the uninitiated, ice or heavy frost on top of the wing is a definite "no-no," for no pilot in his right mind will fly *any* airplane in that condition.) With the ice cleared, the pilot and the lone passenger trudged out and climbed aboard their sagging aircraft.

Shortly after the plane's engine was started, the pilot taxiied south on the ice's surface, then turned north for the takeoff.

"He roared northward, farther and farther; we held our breath, for they weren't getting airborne," said Maureen. "And they never did. They turned around and came back. Maybe the pilot had discovered the loading of the cargo—or its weight—had something to do with it."

"Anyhow," said Maureen, "the plane came back and stopped. They shifted the cargo and another ground crewman topped off the plane's fuel tank. Soon the pilot was ready to try again."

Maureen said she was worried "maybe they should have de-iced the wing again, but no one else seemed concerned" and the plane taxiied south one more time; turned around and came speeding up the river, making the takeoff without difficulty.

The remaining Cessna and its youngish pilot were then ready to board Maureen and the doctor. Maureen sat in the back, slightly relieved to note the cargo next to her was certainly not heavy. It was predominantly Pampers.

The plane took off with no problems and reached cruising altitude easily. Maureen cuddled down with the Pampers boxes and began watching the nearly endless scene of frozen sloughs and snow covered tundra below. It would be thirty minutes before the flight arrived in St. Mary's.

Almost lulled into a stupor, Maureen had begun to increase her level of confidence when the pilot began asking the doctor questions about the St. Mary's airstrip. She heard him say: "I hear it's on a hill and that the updrafts from the Yukon river could be tricky."

"My God!" she thought. "He's never *been* there before?" (Down went the confidence level again.) "And it's *tricky?*"

But the questions didn't seem to bother the seasoned doctor. He casually described the airstrip and the various approaches taken by the small aircraft and the weekly scheduled airliner.

Then the pilot broke out a map and, over the roar of the engine, began asking more questions. This time about landmarks. And Maureen heard something to the effect: "...never flown over the Yukon before."

"Wow, what have I gotten myself into?" thought Maureen, and began checking the pockets of her parka to make sure she had her survival food and matches in their waterproof container. "I kept reminding myself: If we go down, how lucky a kussiak *(an outsider, a corruption of the Russian word 'cossack')* would be to have a strong young Eskimo man and a veteran physician of the arctic as companions."

Of course nothing of an adverse nature happened, but as Maureen said: "It was the longest 'short' flight of my life!" In her remaining five years living on the delta, whenever the scheduled airline flights were grounded, she stayed home.

Perhaps as passengers, almost all of you must have given an occasional thought about "just how good was the pilot," but it's likely you were more often concerned over "what would happen if one of the engines stopped working." (Those of you who travel with "purpose but not with pleasure" may think of that possibility more frequently.) Any who think it is a problem—psychological or not—have it on their mind and might fear flying because of it.

Of course telling you to forget your fears isn't likely to make the worry disappear. But here is one substantiating reason why such a fear is not the bugaboo it may have been forty, fifty or sixty years ago. The engines on the early airliners wore out mighty fast. Using each of them for 600 flight hours without an overhaul was considered to be a very acceptable utilization.

Can you give us a guess on how long the most modern jet engine is expected to run? Again, without an overhaul?

Would you believe:
- a) 1,000 hours?
- b) 3,500 hours?
- c) 5,000 hours?
- d) 10,000 hours?
- e) 20,000 hours?

Maybe you took a wild guess and came up with the correct answer. As Mr. Ripley might have said in his famous "Believe it or not" cartoons, the answer is: Over two years of *continuous* running!...a figure well in excess of 17,520 hours!

But all that is a far cry from the success of yesteryear's airliners. *Their* engines were good, too, but obviously not *that* good.

In fact, the Sikorsky amphibians built in 1935 and '36 had two engines. Probably the best engines of their day. But even engines have bad days.

Early in 1941 Captain George and his new copilot, Howard, found themselves with one of those days. They had no sooner taken off—less than 500' in the air—when ka-BLOOEY!!.. a major part in one engine chewed itself to bits.

When it did, the power behind that one propeller virtually disappeared, but the plane's remaining engine kept them safely airborne.

In keeping with the best interests of safety, however, George wasted no time in getting that plane headed back downwind for their emergency landing at their departure field. And Howard was busy calling the field to let them know a problem existed.

At the time George didn't feel he had such a worrisome situation that he had to do much more than simply fly the airplane. He knew one engine could keep the plane airborne. George passed over the edge of the small town adjacent to the airport; wheeled into his approach and began his descent to the runway.

He was thinking about what had probably happened to that big, useless engine that had quit giving him power. George was pretty sure it had been a failure of what we called "blowers" in the engine mechanism. When they were working right, those blowers were gadgets that did a good job of providing extra power, but they had to be treated with considerable respect. George had been flying those same planes for seven years and knew just how to care for the engines, but this one finally wore out. (They were well known for being the first part to wear out, and this one did it up in style.)

As George quickly brought the plane around to final approach, both pilots were startled—and mighty thankful—to see all of the town's fire trucks mustering right there on the airport. (Back in those days crash crews and fire trucks weren't in anybody's airport budget.)

Immediately after the landing and still on the runway, the pilots couldn't wait to radio the airport station manager and extend their appreciation.

"Sure did a good job in getting those fire trucks here so quickly!"

"Hey," responded the station manager, "by the time I called them they had already left the station house and were halfway here. When you lost that blower, you had a trail of flame 200 feet behind the engine and a plume of black smoke half a mile long! Everybody in town could see it!"

Both pilots were plain thankful they hadn't been able to see the fire and smoke. They might have died of fright!

Sure.. it's been said before: Good flight attendants have that public relations touch. And the one in mind—we'll call her Susie—had developed great customer relations skills.

Of course she copes with the best kind of people in easy harmony; exuding smiles, helpfulness and sincerity. She handles the rather crude, the tactless and the rude with such grace one might think nothing upsets her—often with a wry touch of humor.

But there was a trip out of Anchorage, Alaska, when she got her nose out of joint as a result of a conversation one of her passengers had initiated.

Susie didn't loose her cool with the passenger, she lost it when an erroneous part of the conversation became known to all the rest of her cabin crew.

A young, smartly-dressed blonde was among Susie's passengers. Shortly after imbiding in a drink or two, this young lady sauntered back aft to Susie's galley and started small talk.

"Then she got serious," said Susie. "She made a surprising comment." (Assuming Susie was far beyond her youngish 40+.)

"You should be retiring soon, right?" popped the passenger. "I mean, you *do* have to retire at 65?.. not that you *look* 65."

"Well," Susie admitted, "I was quite taken aback by that observation." It was then Susie compounded the passenger's misconception by executing a cheerful, appropriate `put-on'. Without hesitation Susie decided to make some fun out of it, and said:

"No, actually we don't have to retire until we reach 70, but I've had two facelifts already, *(Reality: 0 facelifts)* so I have a way to go."

The passenger was taken in. Her jaw dropped and she said: *"Two facelifts!* Wow! You really look terrific! You don't look 65 at all!"

Susie was smiling to herself and rather pleased to have come up with such an intriguing comeback to the passenger's comments.

It was only later Susie realized her little story had been overheard by one of her fellow flight attendants. Susie's "age" was all over the airplane! Another of the crew entered Susie's area and said:

"Susie.. I didn't know you were 65!"

Whattt?.. I'm NOT 65!"

"But Mac just told us you were.. he heard you tell that to a passenger."

"Oh my god!" exclaimed Susie, "I was just *kidding* with that passenger. I'm NOT 65!"

So far, none of Susie's compatriots have started calling her 'Grandma.'

At least, not without a smile on their face.

Speaking of smiles.. There were lots of them another day when Susie's flight made an intermediate stop.. a stop that lasted a minute less than she would have liked.

Susie, in her usual helpful fashion, spotted an elderly passenger trying to leave the aircraft with a terrific array of hand baggage.

"Okay, I'll give her a hand; she's got a long walk ahead of her," says our gal, and so informed one of her compatriots.

Apparently it was a rather slow walk to the front of the terminal. Suddenly, she became aware the outgoing load of passengers were all boarded. She had to "move it."

As luck would have it, the plane was "buttoned up" before Susie could make it back to the gate. Reaching the entrance to the loading bridge, Susie hears the jet engines turning. The doorway to the bridge is already closed and she starts beating on the door hoping the station people on the loading bridge would hear her and open up.

No way! It doesn't happen.

Now the whining spin-up of the jet engines tells her the plane is pulling away from the bridge! No one had remembered to tell the captain of Susie's momentary absence.. now that absence looked permanent!

"My god! They're going to leave without me!" She knows she's in *big* trouble. Technically, the airline will be in violation for not having enough flight attendants aboard. And it's her fault!

Susie rushes to a window. Sure enough, the airliner is pulling out of its parking place. *Actually leaving her!*

No sooner had the plane left the loading bridge, it suddenly became apparent to the cabin crew that Susie wasn't aboard. In the time it took getting word to the captain, he was out of the terminal area entering the departure taxiway.

In the meantime, the station crew had met Susie. They got off a quick radio message to the aircraft confirming her absence. The captain knew he couldn't leave her. He may have been upset, but he turned around and came back to the parking spot ready to mate up with the bridge.

Susie, filled with anxiety and red-faced over her goof, came aboard to smiles and applause all around. She hurriedly took her proper place and knew, by the rather raucous appreciation of the passengers, the captain was unquestionably aware of her return.

Of course there are days like that when you'd just as soon forget 'em. And when the things that go awry reflect upon your profession, you'd like to be someone else.

But some pilots do other jobs within the company, if they are asked. One of the more common opportunities for a pilot to earn extra greenbacks is to become a company check pilot. (A check pilot is one whose flying expertise and his knowledge of the regulations are excellent; he has ability to transfer his knowledge to other pilots, and to act as an instructor or to check up on the current capability of others.)

But that wasn't the type job Captain Con was asked to do. In addition to his flight duties, he had been offered the chance to become a TV "pitchman" for his company.

Years earlier, this particular airline bought the idea that TV commercials can really sell. Officials realized the public's view of an airline pilot was a person with charisma. Hence, if he or she is seen on TV or in visual advertising, the airline itself had some charisma. In past years this one company used Captain Joe as their first media man. Joe, who always looked his handsome best, left the limelight when he moved off into retirement.

Con fit the bill quite well and proved to be a good choice. He had that down-home, friendly look and spoke with a nice clear, gentle voice.

Of course on TV, Con was usually seen dressed in his uniform. It wasn't a great surprise to find a lot of TV watchers who began to know him as "that pilot on the TV."

Don't forget now.. Con did all that TV stuff and still had to fly. (He didn't want to give up flying for any glamour job.) Con had two habits not every pilot would copy. One was always being friendly and the other was opening his cockpit door after arriving at the terminal. He'd sit in his seat and turn halfway around to watch all the passengers walking forward to the main exit doorway. If they wanted to take a quick look inside, or say something to Con, it was okay with him.

Many of his flights covered the same route every other day or so. One lady took the trip often, but if she had flown with Con before, she apparently had never bothered to look him over.

One day Con left the big city with a load of travelers and this one particular lady happened to be aboard. It later became pretty obvious she was one of the many who had seen Con on TV.

In short order Con and his 122 passengers arrived at this lady's destination. Unfortunately the landing was as hard as week old toast. Even a couple of seasoned flight attendants had to look at each other and raise their eyebrows over that one.

When the plane got to the terminal and tied up at the loading bridge, Con bravely did his usual thing: opened the cockpit door, and turned in his seat ready to wave or smile a 'goodbye' to any of the passengers who cared to peer into the cockpit.

Of course, he never mentioned the landing.

He didn't have to. That lady passenger did it for him. She said it all.

She peeks in the cockpit quickly, does a double-take, then says to Con, the star of TV commercials:

"Ah ha! I thought so!" she says very seriously, "you're really just an actor!!"

Nothing new about finding a woman in an airplane cockpit today, but years ago it just wasn't possible to find a lady riding high in the "front office" of an airliner.

And finding the cockpit door open during the loading process of a DC-9 is not too uncommon, either. One of the author's friends is "out of the old school" and he sure didn't want to look through that door to find one of the female sex sitting in the cockpit. Like he once said: "The day I walk aboard an airliner and there's a blond ponytail sittin' in the captain's seat, that's the day I turn around and walk right off the airplane."

Well, he wasn't alone. It took the macho male types some time to adjust.

But for several years now, the female captain has been there and doing well.

A good example from the very beginning was Sherry, a lady who skippered the first all-female crew on a scheduled airline back in 1979.

Sherry was the initial female pilot hired in this one particular airline. And she didn't press her luck. During her first year of probation she bent over backwards to avoid even looking much like a woman. She kept her hair up under her hat, wore no nail polish, and did away with makeup. Somebody suggested she might even have been trying to lower her voice.

Of course all that didn't keep Sherry from being hassled by some of the male pilots. Especially after Sherry and her husband had figured out that families don't really exist until there's a baby around. In any case, Sherry found herself pregnant.

In six months the uniform just didn't fit too well and Sherry whipped up some special shirts that wouldn't change the shape she was in, but they would cover the situation.

The modification was fine for Sherry, but technically it did not satisfy the pilots' uniform code which states: "The shirt is to be neatly tucked in at the top of the trousers."

Of course that didn't work for Sherry. She had her shirts hemmed straight across just below the belt line and there was no way they could be tucked in. Besides, everyone with an ounce of sense knew the pilots' uniform code was written for males by males.

Sherry's good sense prevailed except in the eyes of one smart alec. He had to open his mouth and give her a bad time about the non-reg shirt.

Just as the shirt had done, most people around that airline thought Sherry's response covered everything pretty well:

"Listen, buddy, when you get yourself knocked up, you can wear your shirt just like I do."

And she's still at it. Flying, that is.

Another pilot who has developed skill is Irwin Malzman. Been flying his helicopter for years.

He was up doing his morning traffic watch for Honolulu's radio station KSSK when he couldn't resist getting caught up in some criminal activity.

Habitual TV watchers of the good guys against the bad have heard the gunman's phrase "I'll blow you away!" On the morning Irwin got himself involved, he did something like that. But he did it with something less violent than a gun.

The whole incident took place on the Ala Wai Canal, that body of water separating Waikiki from the rest of Honolulu. Malzman was airborne when his radio picked up a police report about a lawless character having earlier stolen a canoe and currently just leaving the scene of another attempted burglary. The suspect left because the gendarmes were already upset over the canoe and eager to put the arm on him.

Turns out the 'no-good' had parked his canoe on the canal bank to make this second attempt at brazen criminality. But with the cops hot on his heels, he piled back into the canoe and furiously paddled away, leaving the 'good guys' running up and down the edge of the canal in a futile attempt to capture him.

That's when Malzman really got involved. He picked up one of the police officers and twirled his chopper out over the center of the canal and dropped down over the fugitive's canoe.

Virtually sitting atop the bad guy, Malzman really didn't need his passenger's help to whip up a heavy downwash of wind from the blades of the chopper. Malzman literally blew the canoe and its occupant against the canal's shoreline—and into the waiting arms of the guys in blue.

Speaking of helicopters and skill, an interesting and ironic example occurred off Honolulu's shoreline in the summer of '96.

A local Honolulu flight training school got themselves geared up to make a promotional TV film involving the school's aviation program. Theirs was oriented toward fixed wing aircraft, (the way the author heard it) but they were using a 'copter as a camera plane..

a 'copter they had rented. A shiny, four-place Mooney was one of the target ships of the camera crew. Perhaps an accompanying twinengine bird had a part in this video, as well, because it was airborne and in close company.

Of course, the real action for a film on flying is always doing something in the air, and that's where they were.

When the camera started running, the chopper moved in for a close-up. The chopper got *real* close! When the scene was done, the helicopter pilot must have pulled sharply away, swinging his tail rotor wide and toward the Mooney. The Mooney's wingtip got nicked badly.

The filming might have gone well up until then, but it won't be continuing soon—not with that helicopter, at least. Without its tail rotor to provide directional control, it spiraled slowly downward into the sea. The Mooney flew home without further trouble, its crew deeply concerned about the fate of those in the 'copter.

The crew in the 'copter suffered no injuries, but certainly they had more than a dampening of spirits.

On occasion some of us have allowed ourselves to be talked into an airplane ride with a pilot of questionable capabilities. When it happens, it's easy to get the squeamies. (It's damned easy when the plane is continuously bumping along inside storm clouds.)

The well qualified pilot-passenger knows not all pilots have the skills and experience to fly solely by use of the cockpit flight instruments. The guys may know the theory, and they may have hours of flight time but do they have the expertise? Sometimes we don't discover the truth until we're thousands of feet in the air. Worse yet, when we're buried in clouds.

All fliers have initiated thoughts of doubt when we're flying with a pilot whose level of experience is less than what we might call adequate. The essence of that doubt (in pilots and in passengers) is:

"I sure hope the pilot knows how to handle this situation." (And just possibly the doubt is passed along to that Great Dispatcher upstairs asking for some help—if the pilot needs it, of course, because we'd never *think* of interfering.)

So it was with long-time friend Don when he was an "airplane driver" for the Navy. He was quite knowledgeable about what we call instrument flying. While stationed in Washington, D. C., the two of us would take every opportunity to get airborne over the airways in a twin-engine Beechcraft and look for stormy weather and a chance to practice.

By the time of this story Don was living in Jacksonville, Florida. On a trip to the nation's capital, he didn't rate having his own aircraft; he had to travel as an aerial hitch-hiker with some other Beechcraft pilot. To get back to Jax he had to go the same way. As you know, when you're out scrounging for anything free, the results might not always be precisely what you'd desire—if you had your 'druthers.

In this case, Don accepted a ride with two pilots he did not personally know, but if he wanted the ride, he had no choice but to take their competency on faith. The degree of faith was predicated on his need to get back to Jacksonville. Each of his pilots were senior officers.. both *theoretically* qualified to do what their flight plan called for.

"But the weather wasn't too gorgeous," said Don, "so that gave me some concern. On the other hand, I had to get back and this flight seemed to be my only choice."

"Besides," he stated, "you know how the "Beech" is set up—the cockpit and the passenger section are almost togetherness itself. By sitting in the front of the cabin, I could always read the gauges (the "flight instruments") as we're tooling along." And the rest of his thought hinged slightly on the fact Navy Beechcraft planes were always fully equipped with parachutes and the harnesses that made the 'chutes usable.

You get the picture. My friend knew if one or both of his pilots weren't handling the plane successfully, he could either offer to help or simply bail out.

Before the problems began, that was the setup.

Soon after takeoff, the aircraft began experiencing turbulence and stinko weather which necessitated flying within the clouds. The critique by the pilot-passenger began.

After almost an hour, Don reported "We were still very much in heavy weather and I had yet to see examples of confidence or competency in either of these pilots. Overhearing some of the radio reports to ground stations and the statements of uncertainty from the officer trying to do the navigating, I got into my (parachute) harness." Apparently, the only other passenger felt nervous about the flight, as well, for he quickly donned his.

Finally Don made direct contact with the pilots, and either asked if he could offer any assistance, or was invited by the copilot to provide some. In any case, Don quickly made it known he was "pretty well qualified" to lead any effort toward making the flight a success. With that the copilot asked if Don wouldn't take his place and "try to determine where they were."

"Wow! Did I jump at that opportunity," said Don with great emphasis. "With that, the copilot got out of his seat; stepped back in the cabin and said: 'Here.. give me your harness.' I almost balked at that, because I saw his own harness lying in a tangled mess on the cockpit floor. But I couldn't wait to get up in the cockpit and learn what we had to do to get oriented and back on track."

Don reported both the pilots were "in a mess. They had no idea where they were." Once he learned from his own efforts they were closer to Birmingham, Alabama, than they ever were to Savannah, Georgia, or Jacksonville, Florida, (where they should have been) he asked the pilot if perhaps he didn't need some relief at the helm. That offer was accepted and Don decided to land in the Alabama capital and refuel.

He did, and his original cohort in the passenger cabin must have had a sudden change in heart about going on to Jacksonville.

He couldn't get off the plane fast enough.

A Sikorsky S-43 amphibian
Newer; more graceful than the S-38
on page 181

GROUND TO AIR AND BACK AGAIN

Any bargain is a shopper's delight. And a great many pilots are bargain-hunters, which is a tactful way of saying they squeeze more dimes out of a dollar than the average wage earner.

Some years back a pilot acquaintance was a traveler in what is a shopper's paradise any day of the week—Los Angeles. While he was there on company business, he chose to make the most of it.

Because this fellow was involved in refurbishing his house, he'd found just the store in California that offered a special price on glass mirror tiles. You know the kind.. they are most always a foot square... people paste a wall with them, or whatever. Makes the room look bigger.. classier. It was to his financial advantage to buy about a hundred.

This ardent shopper had finished his airline duties and was ready for the long flight home. The departure time for his flight was three hours away, but the sale of the mirror tiles was happening in a store twenty-five miles across town.

He couldn't pass up the sale price. It was too good. He'd go for it!

He hurriedly checked out of the hotel and zoomed off in his rental car. Fighting traffic all the way, he accomplished his mission, returning to the airport with the fragile tiles. Getting that car back to the rental agency was his last hurdle.

He arrived with only minutes to spare. Quickly removing the small amount of baggage and the rather bulky box of glass tiles from the rear of the vehicle, he set his belongings on the pavement.

Then holding his rental contract; he handed the keys to the lot attendant, and said: "I'm late. Fill it up. I'll be at the counter."

Eager to please, the rental agent jumped behind the wheel; reversed toward the gas pump, and...

Backed over the tiles!

Reliable help is always hard to find, it seems, and going on that assumption, it leads us right into another story.

A pilot is always one who has a great interest in knowing the weather. He or she wants all the details:

WIND: How strong it's blowing and from what direction it comes.

VISIBILITY: The distance in miles one can see on the ground with prevailing weather conditions.

CEILING: Height of the cloud base in feet above the airport. Usually pilots want an altimeter setting, too—the barometric pressure at the field. All those things and more are available at airports that have an official FAA tower.

But airports without FAA control towers usually have a radio service called a Unicom—an unofficial line of communication from the ground to any pilot who might call. Generally, information received from a Unicom cannot (in a manner of speaking) be "guaranteed." Technically, the operators are not "rated" as qualified air traffic communicators, though most operators of a Unicom radio soon learn the pilot-type lingo. Not having learned it is the key to this story.

Up in Wisconsin one day, the Johnson Wax Company had sent a corporate plane to a small, local, non-controlled airport whose only radio equipment was Unicom. The aircraft was not yet in sight of the field when the pilot called on the Unicom frequency to learn what the airport weather conditions were.

The Unicom station's response made the pilot immediately aware the voice he was hearing was not the usual, knowledgeable lady. The 'regular', it turned out, had met with some problem that called for a replacement "talker." This new lady on the microphone had no knowledge about aviation weather, and barely knew more than how to switch her microphone to "on."

The pilot recognized she would need a little help, so he began to phrase his questions carefully.

"I'd like a report on the wind.. can you look out the window to your left and tell me which way the orange windsock is pointing? Is it hanging limp?.. or standing out straight because of the wind?"

This novice lady looked to her left and said: "It's limp."

Good, thought the pilot. He knew wind wasn't going to be a factor.

Next he wanted a report on the visibility and knew she would need help to understand that question. He was well acquainted with all the major hazards in the area of the field, so he asked her if she could see the top of a specific mountain some two miles or so away.

She reported back a simple "Yes," so now he knew the visibility was at least a mile.

Of course, he still hadn't found out if there were clouds above the field and what was the ceiling.. that is, the height of those clouds above the ground. He must have momentarily forgotten he was dealing with a rank newcomer in airfield communications, because he asked her:

"What do you estimate the **ceiling** to be?"

She paused just slightly, then came back with the answer: "Acoustical tile."

Absolutely no transition could be developed for a follow up to that tale, short of saying both stories include aviators and females.

There is always some chemistry thriving in the workplace. The male/female one you know all about, but another test-tube full is the urge to pull an occasional trick on a fellow employee.

Maybe both of those "chemical elements" made it easier for a certain flight attendant to become an indirect accomplice to some petty larceny.

Our "stewardess" (Was that before your time?) spent her morning tending passengers while the plane bounced from one airport to another, our little lady working the small cabin solo, as was usual for the aircraft type.

The twin-engine airliner's crew of three was scheduled to spend the day together; ten landings in all. The stewardess was typically attractive, young and smilingly hospitable. The pilots up front had personalities as different from each other as the Creator could have made them. The captain, far from being staid, was a serious prankster. Over in the right-hand seat, the copilot was disciplined, regulation oriented, and wore his well kept uniform with great pride.

As it should be, the copilot hadn't been around the airline as long as the captain. The captain knew things his cockpit helper didn't, and that slightly superior knowledge wasn't all limited to flight experience.

For instance, the captain knew the stewardess with whom they were flying had a hobby collecting airline pilots' wings and emblems from the uniforms they wore.

That captain planned to make a small contribution to the collection. But it wouldn't be something taken from his own uniform.

When the copilot had stepped aft to use the plane's facilities, he left his hat displaying the airline's handsome porcelain crest. The captain, seizing his opportunity, quietly removed the crest and slipped same in his pocket.

It wasn't long before the surprised copilot discovered he had somehow lost the beautiful pair of wings that had earlier been perched so properly upon the brow of his uniform hat. The copilot wasn't very happy about his loss, and never truly sure a moment of unusual carelessness of his own hadn't been the reason.

He searched that plane from stem to stern. Irritated at being out of uniform, the copilot never learned he had been the target of a "larcenous" captain. And now it was his own obligation to buy another crest to adorn the bare brow of his hat.

In the meantime the captain had palmed the small emblem into the stew's hand, saying: "Here's something for your collection."

This happened some 40 years ago when flying in the old propeller-driven Douglas DC-3 was probably the safest way to fly.   It just wasn't altogether safe for your hat.

Flight attendants usually have a "giving" manner. They enjoy pleasing people. They have to, or they would find boredom in their work. This story has a particular twist to it that seemed worthy of your time.

Probably not too unusual for a large group of folks in the U.S. to charter a jumbo jet to visit their ancestors' homeland. Happens all the time. They probably enjoy it. Possible, however, on this one particular trip they didn't enjoy their meals as much as one of their captains appreciated his.

As might be expected (if you've ever taken the more common charter trips) it was all done at the most reasonable price. No doubt the plain, workaday Yankees who took this charter flight had no expectations of dining on special or catered meals.

The flight originated in California. It carried a large group whose ancestral background lay in the Azores, the Portuguese islands situated in the eastern Atlantic Ocean. Of mutual heritage and living in Massachusetts, were those remaining passengers due to be boarding when the aircraft stopped for fuel and a crew change in Boston.

The stop in Boston would provide the inbound crew from California a day or so to rest up before they re-boarded the aircraft for their return to the west coast. Once the big jet returned from the Azores, they would again be back at work.

In command of the original crew that had flown east out of San Francisco was Captain Joe K. He was well liked by the flight crew, and one of his considerate, thoughtful flight attendants realized it would be Joe's birthday before they all returned to the city by the Golden Gate.

Unfortunately, in Boston on crew rest, there was little opportunity to give Joe a lavish party in that city. If the party givers waited until they completed their long day of flying back to the west coast, the only person likely to be interested in a party upon reaching San Francisco would be Joe K.

Someone got the wise idea "why don't we give him his birthday party on our return flight *to* San Francisco?"

"Hey!.. Why not?" was the immediate reaction. "Besides, having a surprise party on board would make it easy—Joe couldn't get away."

They all agreed. "Heck, we'll just celebrate Captain Joe's birthday somewhere over Illinois; we'll fix him a dinner en route to San Francisco."

They were adamant Joe was going to get a real, number-one New England seafood dinner. Prior to their departing flight, the young ladies (giving up some of their crew rest,) went out shopping for the fancy items they planned to serve to Captain Joe.

The hour finally arrived for Joe and his jet to leave Boston. He was up in the cockpit doing his usual thing; having no knowledge of what was being planned for him.

As quickly as it was permissible to serve the passengers their meals, it was done. No frills; no culinary delights; nothing very impressive.

Then the girls in the galley commenced working on their big surprise of the day. They had displaced the conventional contents of Joe's food tray and began loading it up with a beautiful, eye-popping gourmet's delight.

Then, in concert and with showmanship, the girls marched proudly through the cabin carrying some magnificent examples of their special talents..

Of course the passengers had heard nothing about a party, and naturally, none of them had been particularly entranced by the meal they had recently received.

So it was nearly impossible for the passengers to ignore the passage up the aisle of a scrumptious entree.. one that would catch anyone's eye:

A large, exquisitely red, Maine lobster.

Airline food is frequently maligned, but when the food is held up for five hours, a hot meal is welcomed no matter what the quality.

And no matter how hard a company tries, all airlines have their share of delays, as in the following story. Yes, delays are bothersome, but since mechanical delays are safety oriented—it isn't worth getting your blood pressure worked up. Try to remember the old airline captain's motto: "If it ain't safe, don't go."

Actually, a special manual, (called the MEL for Minimum Equipment List,) often as large as two big city phone books, tells you precisely whether you fly with your "problem," or if the plane stays on the ground. The MEL is carried aboard every airliner and the instructions in the manual must be obeyed. No matter how small the gidget; no matter how large the gadget... if it needs fixing—follow "the book."

On one occasion a Douglas DC8 four-engine jet was loaded and deemed ready for departure on a military charter. Aboard were the crew, over 200 members of the armed services, plus all the prepared meals the Army men were to be served.

The big jet's engines were already thundering; the captain had received a clearance to the takeoff runway, preparations for departure nearly complete.

Suddenly during the pre-flight check of equipment, a malfunction became apparent. It was a mechanical problem the crew had every reason to believe could be resolved within the hour—two hours at the most.

But it was a malfunction the huge MEL manual clearly defined as one leaving the captain no choice.. he must have the part fixed or replaced before any further flight was undertaken. The plane was taxied back to the terminal maintenance area; the engines shutdown. A further inspection proved the airline not only had a faulty part, they had a faulty estimate for how long it would take to correct the problem. Four hours went by. To keep from losing anyone, all the G.I. passengers were kept on board.

The number one lady of the cabin crew began to fret over the fact all those prepared meals they had aboard weren't being eaten by the two hundred semi-starved soldiers. Had the aircraft gotten airborne somewhere near the scheduled departure time, everyone would have been fed two hours ago.

"Hey...these guys are really hungry," observed the senior flight attendant, and she decided to speed up the program. Her judgement and decision went against the standard company policy, but, she reasoned "we gotta get these guys fed."

She proceeded to take the responsibility and told the remainder of the cabin crew her decision. "I don't know for sure how soon it will be before takeoff, but get started heating some of these meals now." And forty-eight defrosting meals in their foil covered plastic dishes were locked in the two ovens to get their heat treatment. Once the meals were fully heated, the ovens were unlocked; the oven doors simply left ajar.

The sudden but familiar whine of jet engines being started caught the cabin by surprise. Quickly they were notified to be ready for takeoff. Rapidly making last minute seat belt checks on all their passengers, the cabin crew popped into their own seats, secured their safety straps and prepared for go.

Two of the flight attendants sat in their assigned seats facing the plane's ovens. Seconds after the ladies had strapped themselves in, the forceful surge of four jet engines at full power gave immediate acceleration to the big jet. It literally bolted ahead.

In the haste of departure, the oven doors had not been secured, and forty-eight hot meals bolted the other way!

As the plane raced down the runway, those doors fell open and hot meals—two by two—rained out of the ovens, cascading onto the laps of two flight attendants busy shunting aside the heated onslaught.

Any previous concern for proper procedure or patriotic compassion for hungry soldiers suddenly became non-issues.

Civilian airliners have been chartered many times for movement of troops, but only a very few of those flights impose a scared-as jackrabbits condition upon the flight crews.

Each of us have read how Israel and various Arab countries reach a peace accord every so often. It happened again in 1985. Part of the deal involved a United Nations charter flight bringing Fijian "peace keeping" troops into the Sinai desert. The group was to be replacements for other Fijian soldiers already in the Sinai.

The new unit departed their homeland westbound in a Douglas DC-8 airliner. Once beyond the Pacific Ocean, their flight was to make refueling stops at Singapore and Sri Lanka, and overfly several other countries including Saudi Arabia. Their destination was El'Arish, an isolated, ill-equipped, no-services airfield in the desolate desert.

Some foreign nations are quite sticky about the details of flight clearances.. especially when a planned flight asks to make a landing within their borders. And once a clearance is issued, they are adamant that the air carrier "flies by the program."

That situation tends to get worse as one nears the Middle East. Animosities existing between Arabic states and Israel create unseen dangers even to flights *routinely scheduled* to penetrate the airspace of either. To venture forth without proper permits or to violate the clearance initially approved is an unspoken willingness to become "target-for-the-day."

In 1985, standard procedure to obtain a clearance to overfly Saudi Arabia required twenty-one days advance notice. In this instance, the operational planners for the flight of the Fijians had supposedly met all their obligations. And everything went well—up until the aircraft boldly flew west to enter Arabian air space.

There, on the longest leg of the trip, began a merry-go-round of frustration and confusion. When the captain of the aircraft called for his expected clearance to fly over the Arabian peninsula, he was asked for his control clearance number, a series of digits cautiously granted by the Saudis. The captain responded with the only number he had been given. The return reply was alarming—his control number had only been good for the preceding month. As bad luck would have it, a current clearance to fly across the Arabian peninsula had inexplicably "dropped through the cracks." The Saudi's had no record of such a clearance. In essence, the ground-bound flight controller said: "No number; no flight-seeing the sands of Arabia."

The captain was trapped; his destination was on the distant northwest corner of the Arabian peninsula. He had no clearance to land, and no permission for an overflight. Without the Saudi's clearance to overfly, El'Arish was literally out of reach with the fuel remaining.

However, the air traffic controllers graciously granted the captain permission to enter a long holding pattern over Bahrain—an elongated circling flight path at a given altitude over the western edge of the Persian Gulf. From there he made radio calls to everyone who could pass messages back to his operations dispatchers in the U. S., and especially to anyone who could make contact with a Saudi embassy. There *had* to be a way to get a clearance.

Even an element of religion stood in the captain's way, for it was the season of Ramadan, an annual Moslem holiday. Like holidays in many countries, officials—most of all—will take holy days off.

Time passed. With no new clearance and the DC-8 rapidly running out of fuel, a landing was obviously required. Subsequently one was approved. When the aircraft had landed and taxied to its assigned location, it was immediately surrounded by a cadre of armed soldiers.

While the atmosphere was quite warm; the welcome would have been appropriate for a polar bear. The armed guard made it clear no one could leave the aircraft until their inspection team was satisfied no weapons were aboard; then, only the captain could debark.

The menacing attitude of the Arab welcoming party was such the captain realized how fortunate he and his crew were that his load of troops were not armed. Fortunately, the new Fijian group had planned to perform their desert duties using weapons already in the hands of the troops they were to replace. The captain deduced—and no one seemed to doubt him—he, his crew, and the Fijian soldiers would have all been shot had weapons been found on the aircraft! It was scary!

When the captain was eventually granted permission to begin his talks for fuel and that all-important clearance, everyone else had to remain aboard, roasting in the now overheated aircraft cabin.

The end product was receipt of a new flight clearance and the aircraft took off. After another 1500 miles, it delivered its "military cargo" to a sun-baked airfield at El`Arish. The crew, lucky to be nearly doubled in size for their hours-on-end aerial adventure, then embarked a new group of soldiers and headed back to Fiji 12,000 miles away.

As is evident from time to time, not every flight is one of happiness. Take Flight 462, a Douglas DC-8 jet, which was still over an hour south of its Honolulu destination when a woman being transported from Pago Pago began having seizures.

Kathy, the flight attendant in charge of the cabin, had realized prior to departure, the woman now in trouble was far from healthy. She had been carried aboard through the forward aircraft service door by three medical attendants.

Getting the stretcher-borne patient into seats B & C in row 14 had been a project, for the balance of the passengers were already aboard.

Prior to their deplaning, the medical personnel had equipped their charge with properly installed intravenous feeding tubes and fluid medication equipment, enough to last the eight-hour flight north to Hawaii. Throughout the trip the support equipment had been functioning as intended. The passenger had lain across the seats, resting her head on her escort's thigh, apparently taking the journey in relative comfort, sleeping peacefully; breathing in the oxygen slowly.

During the previous hour the flight attendant realized there had been a change in the woman's status, she quickly relayed her concern to the captain. He acknowledged the report and asked to be kept updated on the situation. Almost immediately thereafter, the flight attendant hurried into the cockpit with news that one of the passengers, a doctor, felt his own services were needed and was now attending to the sick woman.

Despite the doctor's presence, his capabilities were limited aboard the aircraft and the passenger's condition continued to worsen.

Meanwhile, the DC-8 was still an hour away from Honolulu cruising at a speed of Mach .80 (roughly 550 mph.) The captain had just been instructed that in 15 minutes he should contact Honolulu Air Traffic Control Center. As the aircraft approached the airways intersection named Niemo, contact was made.

At the same moment the situation in the cabin suddenly became more acute; the doctor telling the lead flight attendant their passenger's condition was noticeably worse and he wanted to be sure the captain knew. Further, he believed it was imperative they make every effort to reach Honolulu more quickly.. "increase the plane's speed... shorten the route.. whatever it takes!" Beyond that, to be sure all his information concerning the passenger be radioed to the medical personnel on the ground.

The doctor was obviously worried about how much time remained before the airliner could land at Honolulu. Perhaps there was a closer airport.

Realizing the situation had now become critical, the captain immediately advanced the power of the four turbojet engines to accelerate the aircraft from Mach .80 to Mach .84, increasing the plane's airspeed by another 30 mph. He also had the first officer make radio communications with the Air Traffic Control Center; explaining there was an urgent emergency aboard and the flight was seeking the most direct flight path to the airport.

Center responded and quickly coordinated a route through airspace routinely used only for military training. A direct route shaving ten minutes off the normal route.. a change of major importance in this crucial situation.

Aboard the aircraft, the doctor continued to send medical messages. Either written or given verbally by the doctor, Kathy delivered them to the flight deck, the pilots relaying them through Honolulu Center to the medical personnel on the ground.

Everything that could be done was being done.

Shortly after a high speed descent was begun 170 miles south of Honolulu, the flight attendant brought another note from the doctor to be relayed by the captain. It read: "Allergic reaction to Cortisone, Borderline code 500", implying the patient's breathing had almost stopped, that resuscitation was urgent. No sooner had it been sent through Center when the doctor sent another to the cockpit and it read: "CPR in progress, code 500." In delivering the latter information, Kathy made certain the captain understood the doctor had recommended "we proceed to the nearest airport."

The cockpit crew checked the distances, but determined a landing at Honolulu would be their fastest option. Diverting to any other island airport would take longer.

Within 40 miles of Hawaii's island of Oahu the Center controller transferred flight control and communications to the Approach Control facility at Honolulu.. the flight cleared "straight in" to the runway of the captain's choice. He chose runway 8-left with a short, right-hand approach; the most direct way to a landing, one that would reduce the plane's flight time by an extra minute or more. If there had been low clouds at the airport, it would have meant an extra five minutes in the air.

The landing was smooth, the DC-8 touched down in the first 2,000 feet of the runway and hurriedly taxied into the airport terminal.

Once into the deplaning gate, the aircraft was stopped, its crew quickly opening the service door and dispatching the patient to the waiting medical personnel.

The crew of the plane.. the doctor.. and the air traffic controllers involved had done their best. Their cooperative undertaking had been outstanding. It had been a superb effort.

Tragically, the patient was never able to appreciate it. She died on arrival.

Douglas M-2 of the 1920's...
An aerial postman's dream

FORGIVE US OUR TRESPASSES

If an airliner racing down the takeoff runway suddenly comes to a screeching halt, it's called an "abort." Fortunately it's an event that rarely happens.

An abort can be a shocker because the sudden, shuddering deceleration is traumatic to the passengers. It is decidedly noticeable.. like someone locking the emergency brakes on an onrushing freight train, or a truck driver trying to smoke all 18 wheels of a speeding highway freighter.

An abort occurs because the pilot is suddenly aware he has a problem. *What* it is will be explained by the captain as quickly as possible. Your cabin attendants will follow that message with more explicit details where required.

Of course the pilot's choice to abort is the wisest thing he could do if he foresees trouble ahead. It is a safety precaution created by one of several reasons. Perhaps misdirected traffic endangered the airliner, or the aircraft developed a malfunction.

If an abort happens, the normally smiling, helpful flight attendants quickly brace themselves for an emergency evacuation of all passengers—right there on the runway. In the rare case of that most serious type abort, an immediate follow up to the sudden stoppage of the aircraft is most important, for it truly involves the cooperation and safety of all passengers. Stand ready for instructions. Being at maximum alert is far more important than helping others to panic.

The safety-minded Federal Aviation Administration flight inspectors all look at aborts as serious business. Finding an airliner in the mud off the far end of the runway is one of their big "no-no's." It means the pilot's braking technique was inadequate.

The inspectors know every airliner carrying passengers within the United States and virtually every country in the world can be stopped on the runway using brakes alone. (FAA regulations require that capability before a plane makes use of each runway from which it shall fly.) Those inspectors work hard to make sure pilots know how to do a proper abort. It means practice. Not on you the passenger, but in a flight simulator or, if necessary, in the real airplane, sans passengers.

Sometimes a flight simulator is just not handy when a pilot is being given his or her flight checks. If the only equipment the inspector and the pilots have available is the "real thing," the abort and other procedures must still be performed. They have to meet FAA standards.. to be done "by the book." So the inspector rides in the cockpit with the pilot—no passengers aboard.

Now that you know the procedure, here's our story:

One airline pilot (we'll call him Captain Richard) was scheduled for his upgrading to command a DC-9. His previous briefing sessions with his own airline check pilots reminded him:

"Your FAA inspector is really hot on pilots doing a good job on aborting a takeoff properly. Just keep it in mind. Be ready to lean on the brakes."

"Got it," says Richard.

The day came for Richard's flight under the stern gaze of the FAA's inspector. Richard is in the captain's seat; the plane has been cleared to the runway.. the long one, Richard noted. The takeoff check list had been finished; the anti-skid braking switch was on. Everything was all set and the tower cleared him for takeoff.

"Uh-huh," he says to himself, "right off the bat, this is gonna be the big `emergency abort.' The FAA fuzz is gonna call out an `engine failure or a truck crossing far down the runway', or some damned thing just to see if I can do a good abort."

Sure enough, Richard and the DC-9 are barreling down the runway and suddenly the inspector loudly calls out "Abort."

Well, he didn't catch ol' Richard asleep. Not hardly. Richard instantly backed the engines down to full reverse power and literally stood on the brakes!

That DC-9 stopped like a raging watchdog at the end of his chain!

The inspector allowed as how that was the best damned abort he'd ever seen.

However, the remainder of Richard's check ride was through for the day. They weren't about to do anything in that plane again for several hours. It seems the anti-skid braking system had failed to work as advertised. Richard's panic-type stop had locked up the brakes and blown the two left tires; worn the aluminum wheels down to the axles, and caused the crash crew to dash out to see what all the black smoke was about. It left the airplane sitting idle on the runway; the airline's maintenance boss a little upset, and Captain Richard's upgrading check ride delayed, but Richard was pleased to hear the FAA man say:

"Well, I think we can skip the abort procedure next time."

In the old, old days such a procedure didn't exist. However, the need to change one's mind about leaving the safety of the ground *always* existed—far more frequently than it does in today's world.

Nobody in the days of the Frenchman Louis Blériot ever had to worry much about having to reject a takeoff. When balky or faulty engines cut short the attempts to fly, the slow moving airplanes of the day automatically came to a halt.

Yet, even some of our first passenger-carrying aircraft weren't equipped with brakes. And we're not speaking about a plane that uses water as its base of operations, but a regular, wheeled airplane.

"So how did they slow down?.. how did they stop??"

One, the planes landed at a slow speed, hardly more than 35 miles per hour. Pilots always landed into the wind; the throttles closed, and the propellers barely turning. Wind resistance would cause the aircraft to come to a halt in no time. If a plane moving downwind on the ground had a need to stop, it was simply allowed to turn into the wind.

Two—and the answer as to what stopped airplanes when there wasn't any wind. In essence, they simply sat on their tail. Planes in those days had the standard two wheels up forward. Back aft, a "tailskid." (A tricycle landing gear, as most aircraft have today, was not in vogue.) The tailskids kept the planes' tail surfaces off the ground, but also acted as adequate brakes while dragging across dirt or grass fields so common in those early days.

Brakes were not standard items on aircraft in the years before 1930. Basically, the wind and tailskids worked fine until aviation progressed to larger, heavier aircraft.

But the system broke down a bit when taxiing a twin engine aircraft during a strong crosswind. The pilot could control the steering through use of higher power on the upwind engine; a standard practice even today. But in strong winds, in an aircraft without brakes, it often meant the large amount of power needed to keep the plane moving straight ahead also could mean the plane might be taxiing too fast.

And fast taxiing over a rather rough field made for a bumpy ride. It was simply a hassle that having brakes would have relieved.

Years ago one airline had such a problem and it needed a solution, one that literally ended up in the hands of the mechanics.

The answer was to build a dolly—a set of wheels attached to one end of a long handle. But at the other end, they added a mechanic. He not only became the plane's guidance system, but its brakes, as well. The dolly was designed to prop up the tail, which in turn made the relatively lightweight aircraft quite movable.

After the plane's engines were running, the mechanic hoisted the tail of the plane (for the tail was no heavier than that of today's small airplanes;) slipped the dolly under the tailskid; grabbed the handle and prepared to move. He provided that service all the way to the runway. On days when the wind was strong, returning flights received the same service from the runway back to the hangar.

While it all sounds simple, the mechanic had to know exactly where the pilot wanted to go and where the pilot wanted to stop; the mechanic and his dolly literally steering the aircraft. The braking effect that once had come from a dragging tailskid was no longer there; the use of the dolly had given the plane wheels all around. The mechanic's muscles now did the job by pulling back on the dolly with all his strength.

Unless, of course, the pilot had applied too much throttle to the plane's engines.

Which one pilot did. This one thoughtlessly gave the engines too much power, the propeller wash blasted the hapless man on the dolly with a hurricane-like wind and swirling dust, as well as forcing him into a run. Barely able to stay on his feet, there was no way the mechanic could have stopped that plane if the pilot hadn't reduced power.

The mechanic was furious! When that plane eventually returned, he quickly informed the pilot where he could expect to find that dolly if something like that ever happened again.

Soon, however, it became obvious brakes were a necessity. The advent of heavier aircraft and the eventual development of hardsurfaced airfields made tailskids and brakeless airplanes an undesirable hazard.

And when brakes were installed on *his* company's aircraft, no one was happier than the mechanic with the dolly.

When brakes were installed, they obviously became a part of the landing gear. Here's a story about a plane where the brakes were installed but never really needed.

Even though airline pilots usually have a pretty good head on their shoulders, but every so often one shows up that doesn't put that head to work.

But can you believe two non-working heads in the same cockpit??.. as in the story to follow?

Actually, not putting the old "personal computer" into action has caused several "difficult to explain" incidents over the years. It's amazing when you think about it, for one of the very reasons captains have copilots in the cockpit is to help with the thinking.

This incident happened before thorough training was in vogue. Two pilots were flying the old Sikorsky S-38, an early day twin-engine amphibian airliner. It had a boat-shaped hull and because it had a hand-cranked retractable landing gear, it was capable of operating from land or water. In fact, it was the first known airliner with such a capability; a plane unlike any you see flying today (although there is some action afoot to put a full-sized replica in the air.)

But Igor Sikorsky, the designer, knew those wheels hanging down would be a problem if the pilot wanted to try and takeoff from water. Sikorsky's engineers designed those wheels to be cranked up or down—it became the first real job for the copilot.

The pilots had departed one airport for another a half hour away; raised the wheels, and made the approach to land at their first destination. The landing was brilliantly smooth. Any pilot would have been pleased at such a display of finesse. The nice dried-grass field was, in fact, a big plus, for neither pilot had remembered the most important factor in having a retractable landing gear:

Crank the wheels down before landing.

The landing was so good, however, the Sikorsky suffered nothing more than a scratch. Of course the pilots' egos were crunched for their thoughtless action, not to mention how embarrassing it must have been to find their airplane just couldn't be taxied up to the terminal.

But that wasn't the end of it. Six or seven years later while flying in a newer model Sikorsky, the S-43, those same two pilots almost did a repeat.

"Almost, y'say??"

Yep! The second time it happened at a different field.

And don't ask me where they were working after that day.

Which leads us to yet another story about the landing gear... one that sounds plausible if you know how some captains valued their unquestioned authority.

Some years back a young copilot was scheduled to fly every working day with the same authoritative captain.

Early on the captain gave the young pilot in the right-hand seat the 'word' on how and when every action in the cockpit was handled.

"If anything is moved in this cockpit, I'll tell you to do so. Is that clear?" he stated. "Don't do *anything* until I tell you."

After two months of flying in near boredom, rarely getting a chance to manipulate the flight controls, and verbally slapped on the wrist six or seven times when he suggested an action-issue was at hand, the young pilot finally got the message.

"Dammit," he thought, "I don't care what happens, I'm not going to say a thing!"

All of that determined resolve was well and good for several days. The copilot never gave a hint he was ready to reach for the flaps, make a radio contact or lower the landing gear, but ready he was.. always on the ball to accomplish whatever the captain ordered.

Finally, the inevitable happened. As their flight approached an airfield; the captain readying himself to make a landing, called for some various settings of the wing flaps, radio calls to the tower, etc.

But halfway into the final turn he had failed to order a lowering of the landing gear.

"By God," steeled the copilot to himself, "I'm not gonna tell him!"

Closer and closer to the airport; lower and lower... all the way down to the last half mile of air travel, one hundred and fifty feet above the ground.. *still* no command!

In twenty-five seconds they'd be on the runway sans wheels!

The copilot could stand it no longer. He gave in!

In panic, he blurted to the captain:

"Do-you-want-the-gear-down-now?"

"Nooo," drawled the captain, "not now—**NOW!!!**

There are many memorable stories about pilots who couldn't remember to put the gear down, but here is one that made a captain just *think* the landing gear wasn't in the safe, down-and-locked position.

And it undoubtedly ruined his whole day.

This is rumored to have happened at Houston in the days when Eastern Airlines was still in business and had a scheduled departure simultaneously with a competitive airline.

Each jet left from different areas of the terminal at or about the same time. As usual, the tower's Ground Control unit gave each plane clearance to taxi (by separate taxiways) out to a merging point next to the duty runway.

As both got closer to the runway which had no other traffic waiting or leaving, each of the aircraft called in: "Ready for takeoff."

The controller on tower frequency could see the taxiing planes were close to reaching a point of collision unless one plane stopped, but he took a rather casual approach to the event by asking a general question on the radio:

"Who wants to go first?"

Well, no airline crew likes to just sit on the field waiting for somebody else, and the tower man should have known it was his decision to make.

The Eastern copilot was on his toes; quickly activating his microphone and drawling nonchalantly:

"Ohh.. let Eastern go first," correctly assuming Tower would think one of the competition's cockpit crew had graciously made that generous response.

Tower comes back with: "Roger.. Eastern so-&-so, cleared for takeoff."

As the Eastern plane then rolled right in front of the now stationary adversary, the Eastern copilot, looking directly into the other plane's cockpit; picked up his microphone and subtly asked:

"How do ya' like those apples?"

And the Eastern liner turned onto the takeoff runway.

For those of you who don't know, there are some double-checks to inform the cockpit crew whether the landing gear is down and locked in that safe position. When the gear should be down but is not truly *locked* in that favored position, a rather loud horn will blast through the cockpit. (Generally the horns all sound the same.) Anytime that horn is unexpectedly heard as a plane is on the ground, it is so unusual it becomes a near-panic condition. Like every warning system in an airliner, however, the horn can be activated by the pilot for purposes of testing its current condition.

Obviously irritated at being done-in by the Eastern crew, the opposition crew had their own comeback. Quietly containing their frustration, they waited until the Eastern flight was well into its roll down the runway. Next, they took a microphone, held it near their own landing gear warning horn speaker; simultaneously pressing the 'mike' button while conducting a continuous, lengthy "test" of their landing gear warning horn. The result was a long blast over the tower's radio frequency.

It created a shook-up condition in the cockpit of the Eastern flight, for the blaring horn gave the pilots nothing more to think about than the safety of their landing gear! No one could be certain from which speaker came that career-endangering sound! What they heard was **THE** horn.. that was enough!

Though halfway to takeoff speed, the captain shouts "Abort!" and quickly pops the throttles into reverse thrust and delicately leaned on the brakes! He stopped his takeoff and taxied clear of the runway.

Before further conversation was heard on Tower frequency, the sweating Eastern crew heard a short, subdued comment obviously from "you-know-who" parked back at the far end of the runway.

"How do ya' like *those* apples?"

As the author has tried to make clear, this book's title is a take off on the words: To err is human. Each of us will make our share of mistakes in the course of a lifetime.

Yet the aviation industry is unabashedly intolerant of errors. Still, they happen.. and the embarrassment of the responsible parties is difficult to erase.

And when people of the "hard-nose" type indirectly suffer from their own, or a crewman's, error, you can be darn sure the stain will remain. A pompous individual with "egg on the face" will play hell getting rid of it.

If the following story carries the ring of truth, a pilot with one of our leading airlines is still looking over his shoulder at anyone who snickers in his presence.

Please try to bear with the author on this one, for admittedly it takes a person who has a direct familiarity with airliners to truly understand the depth of our story. If you're not in that category, we'll try to give you a short push in that direction.

Virtually all of the larger planes in service today have a retractable landing gear. All so equipped have a "safe" system.. a "landing-gear-locked-in-the-down-position" security condition. One always in vogue when the aircraft is just sitting around with no immediate need to go anywhere under its own power.

The "system" is nothing more than a set of six- to ten-inch rods of pencil-thickness. When an airplane is being placed in an inoperative condition for any indefinite time, those rods—(we call 'em "pins")—are made to fit in precise holes, one in each of the plane's landing gear structure. Helping to keep people from forgetting those "pins," (at the time the plane is about to fly) each of the three has a long red ribbon that whips in the breeze; supposedly so noticeable no one could possibly ignore their presence. It is standard practice for one of the cockpit crew to be certain those pins are removed (and actually carried inside the aircraft) before the plane leaves the terminal.

When a mechanic or a ground service person has put those pins in place, the aircraft may be towed; the airport could suffer an earthquake.. whatever. The landing gear will not collapse.

Fact: Even if the plane flies in that status, that landing gear will never come up!

Since this story is an airline captain's greatest embarrassment, we'll make up flight names and numbers. One airliner we'll call *Dixie 34*, which is stopped directly in front of our number two aircraft, *Howzit 21*. Both are all lined up on the taxiway, awaiting the tower's clearance for takeoff from Los Angeles International Airport.

Taxi and takeoff checklists are done or ready for the last minute items, and suddenly there is a radio call from *Howzit 21* using tower frequency asking *Dixie 34* to "come up on" another radio frequency.

Dixie 34's response is a curt reply to this effect:

"We're professionals. We just don't come up on unofficial frequencies."

End of unofficial commentary.

Eventually, *Dixie 34* is first in line and cleared for takeoff, *Howzit 21* is right behind. As *Dixie 34* starts its move onto the runway, *Howzit 21* is heard making this request of the tower:

"Advise the professionals in *Dixie 34* their pins are still in."

The final communication in that scenario is one that almost literally paints the nose of *Dixie 34* a burning red:

"Tower.. This is *34* requesting a clearance back to the ramp."

Some pilots just seem to walk into unusual situations like that.. but they hardly ever do it the second time.

Take the Pan Am captain flying a trip over the Pacific in the leading airliner of its time forty-five years ago. Those trips were long because the planes of the day didn't have jet engines; the cruising speed somewhat less than 300 miles per hour.

All that time in the air takes its toll on the traveler and the flight crew, as well. Sometime or another, everyone had to use the lavatories. (Even the captain.)

The Pan Am Boeing Stratocruiser had a very sumptuous facility up forward.. quite convenient to the pilots, the flight engineer and the navigator. But it wasn't meant to be for their exclusive use, the forward passenger section also considered it 'their own.'

One young lady passenger from southeast Asia didn't quite have all of the 'smarts' a person ought to have when one uses a public facility like those in an airliner. She hadn't locked the door after she entered.

The door is the real key to the story. It was a two panel folding door.. one that folded inward, diminishing the inside space of the lavatory as it was being opened or closed.

The captain felt the need for his relief, unaware the young lady was using the cubicle. The door was closed, but it was not locked. He charged ahead in all confidence, opening the folding door little more than wide enough to get his head in, when "Oh-oh!..." he never got a chance to say "Excuse me" or "I'm sorry, mam" before that door was kicked shut so fast it would make a captain's head spin!

And there were two simultaneous screams. One from the young lady and another from the captain. The lady did her screaming from embarrassment, at the same time panic-stricken; her legs forcibly holding the door shut—precisely on the captain's neck!

The captain bellowed loudly because he was in pain. His head was in the lavatory, the rest of him trapped on the outside, the door firmly locking his neck in the entrance!

In viewing the scene, the action was hilarious. The captain kept kicking his feet up against the partition behind him, hollering for the lady to please open the door and let him out. After a few moments of that, he finally got some results; the scared young lady relaxed her forceful leverage and released the captain's neck.

To this day no one really knows if either of the participants ever received the personal satisfaction they originally sought. One thing is sure: the captain treated those folding doors very, very carefully from then on.

As might be expected, once airlines really made it clear they were planning to become big business, Big Government stepped in and said:

"Ah..that means we've got to come up with some rules."

And they did... books full of rules. More than we can remember, (at least at the drop of a hat) and rules that do everything nowadays but fly the plane.

In fairness, a safe operation anywhere does need regulation. Yet the longer one stays in the business where those rules apply, the more one realizes all of them made in the name of safety are quite important. (So is common sense, but that element seems *passé*.)

There is one rule that seems rational to every sensible pilot, the one involving the abuse of alchohol. "Loose-use" of alcohol is frowned upon in no uncertain terms.

"For pilots, you mean?"

Yes, but here we're speaking about the passengers. The Federal Aviation Administration has a rule that denies passengers from having more booze than they can handle. (And sometimes that is a tricky obligation to follow.) Another of those rules forbids passengers from bringing their own bottle on board.

Here's a story about an in-flight incident regarding booze.

It was the last flight of a rather stormy night. After the plane had been airborne for a short while, the one flight attendant aboard went up to the cockpit and informed the captain: "There is a fellow aboard who is making his own party and supplying his own bottle."

The complaining cabin attendant hit the captain at a bad time. He had suddenly become extremely busy fighting lightning and bumpy skies. Flying the airplane became much more important than talking. He couldn't risk leaving the cockpit to go back and warn this errant passenger about the rules.

But Bart (he's the captain on this trip) takes just enough time to tell the stewardess to get the passenger's name, which she goes back to do. Turns out the passenger is less than cooperative and tells the young lady:

"You tell your captain I'm the president of this airline."

She figures maybe the statement is true, but she has her orders and passes that along to Captain Bart. Now Bart had been around a long time and he knew darned well he didn't have the president aboard, so he tells the young lady:

"Go back and get his business card. I want to see what his name is."

She succeeds at that, and after Bart finds out the fellow's name— a name he doesn't have any problem recognizing—he gives her instructions:

"Tell that passenger he is breaking a Federal law, and as captain, I'm *required* to call the FBI and to file a report on the incident. If he doesn't put the bottle away, I'm landing at the next airport and calling the Federal officers."

Pretty soon the captain receives a report indicating the passenger had finally put the bottle away.

In the meantime Bart, figuring he had spent enough time on someone who should know better, had already called Dispatch, telling them about the drinker he had on board and gave that passenger's name. He tells the flight attendant to inform the passenger that Federal officers have been notified about this rules' violation.

Upon the plane's arrival at that destination airport, a group of officious people met the airplane. While the passenger wasn't the president of the airline, he did hold an important position in the company.

All that didn't faze Captain Bart one bit. Anyone who bent the Federal Air Regs—especially a fellow who supposedly should know better—didn't deserve any special breaks. Bart demanded the company write the authorities a full report with all of the details.

The airline officials hadn't been aboard Bart's aircraft, of course, and were somewhat reluctant to press the issue. They argued back and forth with Bart for three months, his written report buried away on an official's desk for all that time.

Finally Bart said he would let up if they would schedule the bottle man to one complete day of ground school. The same kind of ground school all flight crew members attend. One that teaches company people what they could and could not do when aboard an airliner.

And that's exactly what happened.

But there's more.

Years later Captain Bart elected to inject himself into an extracurricular career of selling real estate. When he finished his studies, he applied to the realty board for a license. Just like all the other applicants, Bart was scheduled to appear before the members of the board. He had to be approved.

There, big as life and not very eager to give Bart the seal of approval, was the fellow Bart had sent to ground school.

Back in the thirties:
An amphibian to Kailua-Kona—

A child's version of flight in the early 1930's
THROUGH SKY AND SEA VIA SIKORSKY
Barbara Robinson

As our Sikorsky amphibious aircraft slid down the sky, lower and nearer the water, my mother reached across the narrow aisle and patted my knee.

"Don't be scared," she said.

Who could be scared? I thought. My first airplane trip was pure miracle. Of course I knew about the fat turbanned Djinns of Arabia. So they could fly over deserts on their magic carpets? Hah! I was flying over blue ocean—Carter's Ink blue—and close approaching was the Big Island (island of Hawaii) bordered by white ruffled surf.

Down we went, still closer to the water. Hulihee Palace passed by almost beside us. Lower we went—lower and louder and slower. The tops of waves were almost parallel with our windows.

Then suddenly we seemed to nose up slightly and with a mighty WHOOOOOOSH—we were like a fat scimitar cleaving the ocean surface. The sea seemed to fold up and around us, displaying inside it, a glimpse of coral, and darting things, then it flung us up to bob on its surface.

I remained glued to the splashy window scene, blinking at the alternating views of wave tops and mountains. A couple of outrigger canoes were paddling toward us.

Three seats ahead of me the pilot was clicking switches and turning knobs, and then I could hear the water slapping around us. The pilot rose and sidled down the narrow aisle between the passenger seats, climbed a steep ship's ladder and clambered out a hatch in the cabin ceiling.

One by one the passengers wrestled themselves out of their seats, and up the ladder, and disappeared through the hatch; gentlemen first, ladies last. For reasons of modesty, my mother told me.

Then it was my turn. I left my window and gripped my way down the aisle toward the tail. I was used to the ponderous heave and roll of the steamships Hualalai and Waialcale. But this twisting, flouncing, wind-wave motion made me think of Jonah inside the whale.

I emerged from the hatch. The pilot guided my feet down a series of metal foot-rests until I stood balancing on the lower wing, clinging to a slanting wing-brace. The first canoe, carrying four passengers, was already bobbing off toward the dock. Jovial paddlers were maneuvering the second canoe like a sideways battering ram, close alongside, while the pilot, using some of the interesting words I'd learned on troublesome cattle drives, was warding off the canoe with his foot.

Two passengers leaped and flopped from airplane to canoe. My mother stepped in gracefully as a wave lifted the canoe to meet her. Then to the cry of "catch da small keed!" I was tossed over, caught casually by the front oarsman and set in the prow.

Off we went at a leisurely pace. No one looked at a watch.

My Grandmother was on the dock. "Just imagine!" she said. "You left Maui after lunch, and it's not even dinner time yet."

The return to Maui was the reverse. We said farewell on the splintery plank dock, eased ourselves into a canoe again, and paddled off toward the airplane which was swaying out there ahead of us like a huge winged spider treading the water of Kailua Bay.

Part way out a tall regal lady passenger with a fine-woven lauhala hat and blue feather lei, leaned forward and tapped the number one paddler with her carved ivory fan. Without a word he looked back at the steersman, jerked his chin toward the dock, and without losing a stroke we circled back to our still waving families.

Here at the wave-washed steps a man lowered a huge woven coconut-frond basket to the regal lady. She showed me. I looked. There were two indignant hens netted in the bottom. Again we were on our way.

Hens and people achieved the crossing from canoe to aircraft without dignity, ascended the foot-rests placed variously up the side of the hull, descended into the barrel-like interior and sat. Each seat was a window seat. The waves clapped cheerfully beside us.

Then the overhead engines roared with authority, vibrating the marrow of our bones to a near jelly and we groaned forward, slowly accelerating, planed a long way along the wave tops—the jolting slaps rhythmically increasing in tempo—until at last we seemed to shake free—and there..

There below was the green-white-blue-lavender-red KailuaKona and already we could see ahead the long purple dome of Haleakala.

For the reader who has yet to cast an eye on the wonders of the Hawaiian Islands, Maui is the first island northwestward from the isle of Hawaii. The long-dormant volcano, Haleakala, rises ten thousand feet over Maui's southeastern shore, seventy miles from charming Kailua-Kona and Hawaii's forever fairweather airport.

KNOW SOMEONE WHO'D LIKE TO $AVE A BUCK?

To**AIR** is Human *is ready to lose a page...*

...THIS ONE...

In exchange for this coupon and the special sum of $8.95, OLOMANA PUBLISHERS *will be honored to provide* ONE *additional copy of the book,*

To AIR is Human

postpaid to any post office address within the United States.

NAME_____

ADDRESS_____

_____

MAIL COUPON & $8.95 to: Olomana Publishers

(Expect book within 30 days)   1605 Uluamahi Place

Kailua, Hawaii 96734